W9-CCO-969

I finished this book with an emotion I have rarely felt as a reader and reviewer: regret that it was not longer. *The Big Idea* shows how to do little large, and with mega impact. The authors deserve a prize for giving their readers a maximum return on a minimum investment of time and money. I predict (and hope for) many more *Big Ideas*. I'll be recommending this book to so many people that I'll be doing my part contributing to their church's "fun fund."

— LEONARD SWEET, Drew University,
George Fox University, wikiletics.com

The Big Idea is the best book for church leaders I've read in a long time. It stretched my mind while giving me a step-by-step ministry-altering application. Every ministry leader and church planter needs to read this book.

— CRAIG GROESCHEL, Founder and
Senior Pastor, LifeChurch.tv

The Big Idea is a book you need to read. Whether you adopt all of its ideas or just a few, it will bring increased focus, clarity, and life change to your ministry. For nearly twenty years, my own church has benefited immeasurably from applying just one aspect of their vision (tying our small group curriculum to the weekend message). The team at Community Christian and the NewThing Network give us a model that takes church-wide ministry focus to new levels of innovation and collaboration.

— LARRY OSBORNE, Lead Pastor,
North Coast Church

The *Big Idea* resonates with me to the point of conviction. A challenge to pastors and teachers to quit creating "pew potatoes" by bombarding families and communities in any given week with multiple messages they don't have time to put into action on their journeys as Christ followers. *The Big Idea* offers a start in fulfilling what James desires for us — not merely to listen to the Word, and so deceive ourselves, but to do what it says.

— RANDY FRAZEE, Lead Pastor, Willow Creek
Community Church

Dave Ferguson is a change agent. Every time I hear what he says or read what he writes, it challenges the way I think. *The Big Idea* is an approach to preaching that is as ancient as the parables of Christ, but it will revolutionize the next generation of preachers.

— MARK BATTERSON, Lead Pastor,
National Community Church

The Big Idea is huge. Big impact. Big insights. Big tools. Big practical learnings. The way forward for growing churches to drive home God's truth into all of their attenders each week to grow them stronger in the faith. It's big, fresh, and told in a winsome way by one of America's great young leaders, Dave Ferguson. I always learn when I hang around Dave and the team at Community Christian. I encourage you to do the same through *The Big Idea*.

— DAVE TRAVIS, Executive Vice President,
Leadership Network

THE **BIG** IDEA

The Leadership Network Innovation Series

Other titles forthcoming

THE **BIG** IDEA

Aligning the Ministries of Your Church
through Creative Collaboration

DAVE FERGUSON JON FERGUSON
ERIC BRAMLETT

ZONDERVAN®

ZONDERVAN.com/
AUTHORTRACKER
follow your favorite authors

ZONDERVAN

The Big Idea
Copyright © 2007 by Dave Ferguson

This title is also available as a Zondervan ebook.
Visit www.zondervan.com/ebooks.

This title is also available in a Zondervan audio edition.
Visit www.zondervan.fm.

Requests for information should be addressed to:

Zondervan, *Grand Rapids, Michigan* 49530

The Library of Congress has cataloged the earlier printing as follows:

Ferguson, Dave, 1962-
    The big idea : focus the message, multiply the impact / Dave Ferguson, Jon
Ferguson, and Eric Bramlett.
        p. cm. — (The leadership network innovation series)
    Includes bibliographical references.
    ISBN 978-0-310-27241-0
    1. Mission of the church. 2. Christianity and culture. 3. Church and the world.
4. Communication—Methodology. 5. Communication—Religious
aspects—Christianity. 6. Information technology—Religious aspects—Christianity.
I. Ferguson, Jon. II. Bramlett, Eric. III. Title.
BV601.8.F47 2007
253—dc22
                                       2006025104

Interior design: Mark Sheeres

Printed in the United States of America

CONTENTS

THANKS A LOT! REALLY!

Dave: Sue, thanks for being such a risk-taking partner, a loyal friend, a great mom, and the love of my life. I love you. (I told you if I ever wrote a book I would dedicate it to you!) Amy, Josh, and Caleb — thanks for encouraging me and loving me back. I can't wait to see what God does through you!

Jon: Lisa thanks for being my best friend and a phenomenal mom to our children. I'm still crazy about you and grateful to God for your daily doses of love, strength, and encouragement! Graham and Chloe, you are so much fun. I-C-N-U tremendous possibilities, and I can't wait to see how God breathes life into your dreams.

Eric: Thanks to Kristi, my wonderful wife and the best friend I've got — you're gorgeous! Sadie, Dillon, and Anna are the coolest children in the universe. Thanks for loving your dad! Much love to my parents, Perry and Susan, and to my brother Elic, who has always been right by my side, or at least down the street.

Thank you to the best team in the universe (left). You guys make following Jesus ridiculously fun — just like God intended!

Thank you, Pat Masek. Sometimes on a dedication page the authors will comment, "This couldn't have happened without you." In this case, we really mean it! Without Pat, this book really would not have happened. Thank you for your willingness to accomplish a part of the Jesus mission through us and make sure we got *The Big Idea* written.

Thanks to the NewThing Network churches who partner with us every week to create the Big Idea: Jacob's Well Community Church in Thornton, Colorado; 242 Community Church in Brighton, Michigan; Forefront Church in New York; Reunion Church in Boston; and Village Christian Church in Mokena, Illinois.

Thanks to our good friends at Leadership Network: Bob Buford, Dave Travis, Greg Ligon, and Mark Sweeney. We are so grateful for the platform of influence that you have given us. We promise to steward it wisely. And thanks to our new friends at Zondervan: Paul Engle, Brian Phipps, and Mike Cook. Thanks for your patience and guidance in working with a bunch of rookies.

All our thanks and anything good that comes from the words written on these pages is for Jesus. The Big Idea of our lives is to accomplish your mission!

For more information on the NewThing Network, visit www .newthing.org.

For more information on the Big Idea, visit www.theBIGIDEA online.org.

INTRODUCTION

IDEA OVERLOAD!

As I type the first words of this book, fourteen different windows are open on my laptop. One is my blog so I can tell the world what I'm thinking; the other thirteen are various websites — so the world can tell me what it's thinking. My iPod is recharging and hooked up to iTunes, searching for updates of my Podcast subscriptions so that I can get the latest music and musings from my favorite artists anywhere. My cell phone is sitting on the table, giving me total access to the entire planet and the entire planet total access to me. And the truth is, I love it!

We are being bombarded by more and more information every day. Download some of these facts:

- Every day I get an email from the *New York Times* that contains more information than the average person in seventeenth-century England was likely to encounter in a lifetime.
- As I look at the fourteen webpages open on my desktop, I know that 7.3 million new pages are being added to the visible World Wide Web today — and even more will be added tomorrow!
- While I try to finish this introduction today, one thousand books will be published. And the total of all printed knowledge will double in the next five years.
- If I were to start reading right now and continue reading 24 hours a day, 365 days a year, I would never catch up with everything being written.

- While editing this introduction, I received an IM from my assistant, Pat — just one of the 5 billion instant messages sent today.
- My world is now producing nearly two exabytes of new and unique messages placed in over 260,000 billboards, 11,520 newspapers, 11,556 periodicals, 27,000 video outlets, 50,000 new book titles, and 60 billion pieces of junk mail every year.
- Our world will make available more information in the next decade than has been discovered in all of human history!

I could go on and on — and so could you. You are the one who is being bombarded by more and more information on the radio, on TV, online, and in print. And if you're like me, you love it!

Historically, more information has almost always been a good thing. However, as our ability to collect information has grown, our ability to process that information has not kept up. Decision makers can no longer assimilate all of the information they obtain. This phenomenon caused Neil Postman a decade ago to name our society a "technopoly," in which the information glut is not only useless but potentially dangerous. Why? Because today we spend more time studying information than in the past, leaving us with less time for action. Oddly enough, the Information Age has been named for something that once conferred only benefits but is now increasingly a problem.

> We are being bombarded by more and more information every day. And the truth is, I love it!

And the church of Jesus is now experiencing that problem. We have become a technopoly, known more for our bestselling books (guilty as charged — not the "bestselling" part, just the "book" part), our blogs (guilty again!), our TV ministries, and our radio broadcasts than for our action! In the last decade we have not seen an increase in church attendance in any county in any state in all of the United States with the sole exception of Hawaii. Yet at the same time, *The Prayer of Jabez*, *The Purpose Driven Life*, and the Left Behind series have been some of the biggest bestsellers in all of publishing — not just Christian publishing! The movies *The Passion of the Christ* and *The Lion, the Witch and the Wardrobe* have had wide acceptance beyond Christian audiences, and over 65 percent of Christian music is sold outside of traditional Christian channels. Let's face the brutal facts: Information is not bad. And more information is not bad. And more Christian information is not necessarily bad. But more information that leads to less action is a big, big problem, particularly when the action we desire is to accomplish Jesus' mission.

So what will it take for the church to have the missional impact that Jesus dreamed it would have? It will require that we focus less on information and more on action! How? The Big Idea!

PART ONE

• • • •

Little Ideas or the Big Idea?

CHAPTER 1

NO MORE CHRISTIANS!

What do you expect to happen as you read this book? Be honest now. In fact, I'm going to be honest too and put on the table what I hope I can convince you of in this opening chapter:

1. If you've been calling yourself a Christian, you should stop. Maybe not what you were expecting? It is exactly what you and the church need — forget ever being a Christian again.
2. If you have ever encouraged someone to become a Christian, you should never do that again. Seriously, I hope you will never again ask a friend, family member, coworker, or neighbor to become a Christian.

Why? Because the last thing the mission of Jesus Christ needs is more Christians.

Here is the brutal fact: 85 percent of the people in the United States call themselves Christians. Now, let's pause long enough to realize that's a whole lot of people — 247 *million* people, to be exact. But how are those 85 percent doing when it comes to accomplishing Jesus' mission? Here is what research tells us about people in North America who call themselves Christians:

- Those who call themselves Christians are no more likely to give assistance to a homeless person on the street than non-Christians.

- Those who call themselves Christians are no more likely than non-Christians to correct the mistake when a cashier gives them too much change.
- A Christian is just as likely to have an elective abortion as a non-Christian.
- Christians divorce at the same rate as those who consider themselves non-Christians.
- Even though there are more big churches than ever before filled with people who proudly wear the title Christian, 50 percent of Christian churches didn't help one single person find salvation.

In fact, when the Barna Research Group did a survey involving 152 separate items comparing the general population with those who called themselves Christians, they found virtually no difference between the two groups. They found no difference in the *attitudes* of Christians and non-Christians, and they found no difference in the *actions* of Christians and non-Christians. If the contemporary concept of a Christian is of someone who is no different than the rest of the world, is *Christian* really the word you want to use to describe your willingness to sacrifice everything you have to see God's dream fulfilled? No way.

> The last thing the mission of Jesus Christ needs is more Christians.

This absence of distinction between Christians and non-Christians is a huge problem. But it is not a difficult problem. This is a problem for which the solutions are simple, though not easy. So this book is all about one of those simple but not easy solutions for accomplishing the mission that Jesus gave to his church.

Let's start with a typical Sunday as a family returns home from church. The question posed to the children is the same every week: "So what did you learn today?" And the response is too often the same: (Silence.) "Ummm ..." (More silence.) "Ummm ..." (Still more silence.) "Ummm ..."

Parents have tried to think of different ways to word the question for their kids, but it always comes out the same. "So what did you learn today?" It's not the most enticing question, but it's the question that gets asked millions of times every week during the car ride home from church. And the truth is, if our kids asked us, we might

> We have a huge problem — the absence of distinction between Christians and non-Christians.

give them the same response: (Silence.) "Ummm ..." (More silence.) "Ummm ..." (Still more silence.) "Ummm ..."

How is it possible that so many people, young and old, can respond with nothing but silence to such a simple question after spending an entire Sunday morning in church? Is it too little teaching? Is it too little Scripture? Is it too little application of Scripture in the teaching? What's the problem?

Well, let's review a typical experience at church. Is it too little or maybe too much? The average churchgoer is overloaded every week with scores of competing little ideas during just one trip to church. Let's try to keep track.

1. Little idea from the clever message on the church sign as you pull into the church parking lot
2. Little idea from all the announcements in the church bulletin you are handed at the door
3. Little idea from the prelude music that is playing in the background as you take your seat
4. Little idea from the welcome by the worship leader
5. Little idea from the opening prayer
6. Little idea from song 1 in the worship service

7. Little idea from the Scripture reading by the worship leader
8. Little idea from song 2 in the worship service
9. Little idea from the special music
10. Little idea from the offering meditation
11. Little idea from the announcements
12. Little idea from the first point of the sermon
13. Little idea from the second point of the sermon
14. Little idea from the third point of the sermon
15. Little idea from song 3 in the worship service
16. Little idea from the closing prayer
17. Little idea from the Sunday school lesson
18. Little idea from (at least one) tangent off of the Sunday school lesson
19. Little idea from the prayer requests taken during Sunday school
20. Little idea from the newsletter handed out during Sunday school

Twenty and counting. Twenty different competing little ideas in just one trip to church. Easily! If a family has a couple of children in junior church and everyone attends his or her own Sunday school class, we could quadruple the number of little ideas. So this one family could leave with more than eighty competing little ideas from one morning at church! And if we begin to add in youth group, small group, and a midweek service, the number easily doubles again. If family members read the Bible and have quiet times with any regularity, it might double yet again. And if they listen to Christian radio in the car or watch Christian television at home, the number might double once more. It's possible that this one family is bombarded with more than one thousand little ideas every week explaining what it means to be a Christian. No wonder when the parents ask their kids, "So what did you learn?" the answer goes something like this: (Silence.) "Ummm ..." (More silence.) "Ummm ..." (Still more silence.) "Ummm ..."

MORE INFORMATION = LESS CLARITY

We have bombarded our people with too many competing little ideas, and the result is a church with more information and less clarity than perhaps ever before. But the church is not alone in its predicament. Businesses also get distracted with lots of little ideas and forget the Big Idea. Many marketplace leaders are relearning the importance of the Big Idea in regard to advertising. It was a multimillion-dollar sock-puppet ad during Super Bowl XXXIV that epitomized the absurdity of the advertising during the dot-com bubble. This same era brought us commercials with cowboys herding cats, singing chimps, and a talking duck — all great entertainment, but they didn't convey a thing about the brands they represented. Brand consultants Bill Schley and Carl Nichols Jr., in their book, *Why Johnny Can't Brand: Rediscovering the Lost Art of the Big Idea*, tell us this type of advertising is not effective branding. Schley and Nichols exhort companies to redefine their products in terms of a single, mesmerizing "Dominant Selling Idea." They go on to explain that somewhere along the way, "Johnny" forgot the basics of revealing the Big Idea in an easy, everyday way that cements a brand as top dog in the hearts and minds of consumers without resorting to puffery and shallow glitz. What are businesses learning? That "more" results in less clarity. (And less money!)

> We have bombarded our people with too many competing little ideas, and the result is a church with more information and less clarity than perhaps ever before.

Don't misunderstand — this is not a rant against entertainment or churches that are entertaining. I actually think churches should be more entertaining. But that's a rant for another book. This is a rant against churches (and businesses) that don't discipline themselves to create experiences that convey and challenge people with one Big Idea at a time. Why? Because the lack of clarity that we give our people impedes the church's ability to accomplish the mission of Jesus. "More" results in less clarity.

Dr. Haddon Robinson, in his classic book *Biblical Preaching*, recognizes the simple truth that more is less and challenges teaching pastors to communicate with crystal clarity "a single idea." He says, "People in the pew complain almost unanimously that the sermons often contain too many ideas."[1] Robinson is right on. And it is good news that people are complaining. Their complaints about too many ideas tell us that people in the pew want clarity, direction, and guidance in how to live out the mission of Jesus Christ. We can no longer afford to waste another Sunday allowing people to leave confused about what to do next. So let the change begin! But this change can't be relegated only to the preaching. It also must happen in the teaching of children, students, adults, and families and in the overall experience of church life. How? The Big Idea. And it is one Big Idea at a time that brings clarity to the confusion that comes from too many little ideas.

> It is one Big Idea at a time that brings clarity to the confusion that comes from too many little ideas.

MORE INFORMATION = LESS ACTION

In 1960 when John F. Kennedy was elected president, more than $20 million was spent on the presidential campaign for the very first time. The money was spent so the candidates could deliver their political ideas to the people in a compelling way through the new medium of television. Every year since then, more and more money has been spent to better communicate each candidate's political ideology, with the amount increasing more than 400 percent to $880 million in 2004. You would think that with all that money and all those ideas being communicated in every imaginable format, people would be better informed and more convinced to take action and cast their vote for the candidate of their choice. Wrong! More has resulted in less action. Although the 2004 presidential election saw a slight increase in voter participation from the 2000 election, overall, there has been a forty-year trend of declining voter participation in national elections for U.S. president. Why? In Thomas E. Patterson's book *The Vanishing Voter,* he asks, "What draws people to the campaign and what keeps them away?" He discovered after the 2000 election that despite almost a billion dollars spent to communicate lots of ideas, when surveyed on election day, a majority of people flunked a series of twelve questions seeking to ascertain whether they knew the candidates' positions on prime issues such as gun registration, defense spending, tax cuts, abortion, school vouchers, prescription drug coverage, offshore oil drilling, and affirmative action. Patterson concludes, "I don't believe that voters are more apathetic than they were 40 years ago. I think they are more confused than they were 40 years ago."[2] Sure I vote, but do you know one of the primary reasons I vote? It's so I can say, "I voted." Seldom have I gone to the polls with a strong conviction that I really knew the ideology of each candidate. The main feeling I have in connection with voting is confusion, and confusion does not produce positive action.

Around the Ferguson household you can see how "more" results in less action. Having friends over for the evening usually means a scramble to clean up the house and get things presentable for company. So my wife, Sue, and I start barking out orders to the kids: "Vacuum the family room, dust the railings, put away your coat, pick up your shoes, shut the door to your bedroom ..." What happens next? Usually they stand there staring at us and say, "What?" They are willing to help, but after our barrage of requests, they are overwhelmed and do nothing. Now, my wife says that just the boys and I have this problem and that girls can multitask. Maybe. But I think it's another example of the fact that more results in less action. Experience has taught me that if I want the kids to get something done, I'm farther ahead to give them one task, ask them to check in with me once it's finished, then give them the next task. This is the Big Idea approach. It provides clarity and produces action.

I know that as church leaders we can't control the media and the barrage of information that comes at our people — and we don't want to control it. But what we do want is to challenge our people with the truth of God's Word and insist that it be lived out mission- ally. When we contribute to the bombardment of little ideas, we are implicitly telling our people that not all of God's truth has to be accompanied by obedient action. We are implicitly telling our people that just because they hear the truth doesn't mean they necessarily have to live it out. We are telling our people that what is really important is saying it and not doing it.

> We must challenge our people with the truth of God's Word and insist that it be lived out missionally.

ONE BIG IDEA = MORE CLARITY AND ACTION

I was in a graduate class when I heard the Big Idea explained for the first time. The professor, Jim Pluddeman, challenged my classmates and me by saying that the Bible was written to be understood and applied. He said, "The effective teacher is like a person who takes a strong rope, ties one end around the big ideas of Scripture, ties the other end around the major themes of life, and then through the power of the Spirit struggles to pull the two together." I was just beginning to understand that accomplishing the mission of Jesus would mean focusing on one Big Idea, not trying to juggle compet- ing little ideas.

Jesus did not confuse people with a lot of little ideas. Instead, he presented one Big Idea with a clear call to action: "As Jesus was walking beside the Sea of Galilee, he saw two brothers, Simon called Peter and his brother Andrew. They were casting a net into the lake, for they were fishermen. 'Come, follow me,' Jesus said, 'and I will make you fishers of men.' At once they left their nets and followed him" (Matt. 4:18 – 20).

I can't help but notice that Jesus didn't say to Peter and Andrew, "Come, be Christians." Here's how Don Everts puts it in a terrific little book titled *Jesus with Dirty Feet*:

> *Jesus was not a Christian.*
> *He never asked anyone to become a Christian,*
> > *never built a steepled building,*
> > *never drew up a theological treatise,*
> > *never took an offering,*
> > *never wore religious garments,*
> > *never incorporated for tax purposes.*
> *He simply called people to follow him.*
> *That's it.*
> *That, despite its simplicity, is it.*
> *He called people to follow him....*
> *It is never more*
> > *than Jesus' call: "Follow me"*
> > *and a response: dropping familiar nets*
> > *and following, in faith,*
> > *this sandaled Jewish man.*
> *It is never more than that.*
> *Two thousand years of words can do nothing*
> *to the simple, basic reality of Christianity:*
> *Those first steps*
> > *taken by those two brothers.*
> > *Peter and Andrew's theology*
> > *was as pure as it gets:*
> *Jesus said, "Follow me." And we did.*[3]

When Jesus met someone for the first time, he challenged them with one Big Idea: "Follow me." A Big Idea that was simple but not easy. If Peter and Andrew were asked, "What did Jesus teach you today?" there is no way they would respond like this: (Silence.) "Ummm ..." (More silence.) "Ummm ..." (Still more silence.) "Ummm ..." And if they did, it would not be because they were confused and didn't understand, but rather because they were stunned at the boldness and size of Jesus' request. This Big Idea was very clear, and the call to action could not be misunderstood. The simplicity and clarity of that Big Idea, "Follow me," was what catalyzed a movement of Christ followers into action. And these Christ followers knew what was expected of them and would do anything and everything, including trade their very lives, to accomplish the mission of Jesus.

What about "deeper teaching"? That is what the rich young ruler wanted. He came to Jesus and began to explain that he already knew the commandments — "Do not murder, do not commit adultery, do not steal, do not give false testimony, do not defraud, honor your father and mother" (Mark 10:19) — and that he had obeyed these commands since he was a boy. He wanted more. He wanted a midweek service. He wanted graduate-level teaching. With clarity and simplicity, Jesus challenged him with one Big Idea when he said, "One thing you lack.... Go, sell everything you have and give to the poor, and you will have treasure in heaven. Then come, follow me" (Mark 10:21). The message was clear. It was a call to action. It was a Big Idea that was simple but not easy.

> When Jesus met someone for the first time, he challenged them with one Big Idea: "Follow me."

What would happen if we challenged people in the same way? What if we gave people one clear and simple Big Idea and asked them to put it into action? That is exactly what we have been attempting to do at Community Christian Church and the NewThing Network for the last several years. Every week, we give all of our people of every age and at every location one Big Idea and ask them to put it into action. The challenge is simple and clear — but never easy. That's the Big Idea.

Recently we were in the middle of a Big Idea series titled "Get in the Game" for the adults and "U Got Game" for our Student Community and Kids' City. Kids' City puts every Big Idea into one concise statement, and this time it was "God uses his teams' offering to change the world." It was a powerful series. I received the following email from a mom in our church:

From: Kirsten
Sent: Sunday, November 20, 2005 8:18 PM
To: Dave Ferguson
Subject: "U Got Game" Big Idea

I just wanted to let you know that my kids really, really got a lot out of this week's large group time in Kids' City. It made such an impact on them to know where their offering money goes every week. Each week when they get their allowance on Saturday, 15 percent automatically goes with them to church, but they've never really understood where that money goes. (I guess I haven't been very effective at explaining what "giving back to God" means!) Anyway, when they came home this week after experiencing the Big Idea, they both went in and emptied their piggy banks into the offering bags they made and said, "We have to give it *all* to church. There are orphans in Rwanda that don't have homes. We have to help those kids get a home!" Never mind that we talk about "poor people" around this house all the time, but for whatever reason they "got it" in a way they never had, thanks to the way you presented it in Kids' City.

Thanks!

Kirsten

That same week another mom stopped me in Starbucks and said, "Dave, I have to tell you what happened with my boys — it was the most amazing thing. We were going out to get an early start on Christmas shopping at the mall. When we got to the door of the store, there was a Salvation Army bell ringer with his red kettle and bell trying to get donations. I didn't think much of it. Sometimes I give and sometimes I don't — you know. This time I didn't. But when I got inside the store, I couldn't find my two boys. I

> Every week, we give all of our people of every age and at every location one Big Idea and ask them to put it into action. The challenge is simple and clear — but never easy. That's the Big Idea.

looked around for them, and then I saw them outside next to the Salvation Army bell ringer emptying their pockets, giving everything they had. My two boys gave away their entire allowance! I was pleased but shocked. When they caught up with me, I asked them why they did that. They told me, 'Mom, isn't that what they were talking about at church?' It was amazing." That's the power of the Big Idea.

I asked Jen Pedley how the Big Idea impacted her. Here's what she said:

The Big Idea was the first time in my life that God's Word applied to my everyday, ordinary life. It helped me in a practical, "meet you where you are and don't worry, I'll still love you" way. No one had ever spoken so clearly about what it meant to be a Christ follower (I mean, come on, everyone in my hometown claimed to be a "Christian," but I saw firsthand how much that really meant in many people's lives), why you would even want to live this way, and how to do it.

I never heard the Word of God speak to me personally until coming to CCC. I never saw the point until then. Big Idea teaching

> touches on so many basic truths that even though I had gone to churches my whole life, I had never heard before. When you put God's Word into where people are at today — whew, I was blown away. I still am.

Jen came to Community Christian Church in 2000 and soon made a commitment to be a Christ follower. She was baptized, began doing life with a small group of believers, and joined one of our vocal teams. In 2004 she and her husband, Ken, packed up their kids, leaving behind a job and home to move with a group of people from Chicago to the Detroit area to start 2|42 Community Church. Why? They were committed to the Big Idea of selling all they had and following Jesus to accomplish his mission.

> "The Big Idea was the first time in my life that God's Word applied to my everyday, ordinary life."

THE POWER OF THE BIG IDEA

So what if we took that same trip to church, and instead of hearing lots of competing little ideas, our whole family was taught only one Big Idea?

One Big Idea is displayed on the church website.

One Big Idea is on the cover of the church bulletin you are handed at the door.

One Big Idea is projected on the screen as you listen to the prelude music while taking your seat.

One Big Idea is introduced in the welcome by the worship leader.

One Big Idea is the focus of the opening prayer.

One Big Idea is the theme of song 1 in the worship service.

One Big Idea is supported by the Scripture reading by the worship leader.

One Big Idea is the theme of song 2 in the worship service.

One Big Idea is at the heart of a secular song used as the special music.

One Big Idea and how you can understand it further in a small group is the only announcement.

One Big Idea is explained in the first — and only — point of the sermon.

One Big Idea is reinforced through a video.

One Big Idea is the theme of song 3 in the worship service.

One Big Idea is the focus of the closing prayer.

One Big Idea can be explored even more deeply by going to the "next steps" table and picking up a recommended reading list.

One Big Idea and how to have a conversation with your kids on this topic is the theme of the Kids' City handout given to parents.

One Big Idea is the central topic of discussion at small group during the week.

One Big Idea is the focus of the prayer time during small group.

One Big Idea is reinforced by podcast and/or a webcast later in the week.

(Silence.) "Ummm" would not be your response if you were asked, "So what did you learn?" What the church needs is one unmistakable Big Idea. A crystal-clear Big Idea that calls everyone to act on Jesus' mission.

So why does the church in the United States have 247 million Christians and not nearly enough Christ followers? And why is it that we have access to the best and most thoroughly thought-through theology in all of history yet still aren't gaining ground in accomplishing the mission of Jesus? Could it be that we have forgotten the Big Idea and gotten lost in too many little ideas? Is it because the church of Jesus Christ has not challenged people the way Jesus challenged people — with one Big Idea, simple and clear: "Follow me"?

I no longer call myself a Christian. I no longer try to convert people to Christianity. It's not that the title is wrong but that as a label it has come to mean something far different than what it means to follow Jesus. Being a Christian has been reduced to the expectation of niceness. How pathetic. How boring. How easy. How insignificant. And even that expectation of niceness doesn't have to be fulfilled, because the greater expectation is hypocrisy — the practice of professing beliefs, feelings, or virtues that one does not live out. Who would want to be associated with that?

> I no longer call myself a Christian. I no longer try to convert people to Christianity. I am a Christ follower. I follow Jesus step by step as his Spirit moves me in his community called the church.

I am a Christ follower. I follow Jesus step by step as his Spirit moves me in his community called the church. When Jesus steps, I follow. When Jesus speeds up, I increase my pace. When Jesus slows down, I slow down too. The direction, the speed, and the ultimate destination of my life are determined by keeping in step with Jesus' Spirit. Simple. Clear. Not easy!

CHAPTER 2

COMMUNITIES
OF TRANSFORMATION,
NOT INFORMATION

Just a few years ago, this was the headline in the *Chicago Tribune*:

Corpse Discovered after Four Years

Chicago — For the past four years, many of Adolph Stec's neighbors figured the reclusive elderly man had abandoned his neatly trimmed bungalow to the growing weeds and bushes.

Over time, work crews came by to shut off his water, his gas, his electricity. For years, the mailman bypassed his residence, thinking it was vacant. Once in a while, a neighbor would mow the lawn or knock on the door and receive no answer. But it wasn't until Tuesday morning that the developers who bought Stec's home at a tax auction three years ago finally stepped inside to find a man's body almost completely decomposed in his living room chair. A newspaper from 1997 was at his side.

Police described the remains as "mummified."

"One day about four years ago he said hello from across the yard, and I never saw him again," said next-door neighbor Peter Vella, 66, as he was cutting his front lawn Wednesday afternoon. "The grass in his yard got as high as 2 feet, so for two or three years I mowed his too. I didn't want the neighborhood to go to pot."

For now, it's unclear exactly when he died or the cause of death. Police said their only leads are the newspapers and mail in Stec's home that appeared to be as recent as February 1997, when Stec was 72.[1]

While this story made national headlines, it hit particularly close to home for us in Chicago. We asked many of the same questions anyone would ask:

- How could a man die and not be missed?
- Where were his family members? Friends? Even acquaintances?
- Why didn't anyone care enough to simply check on him?

> This story was a painful reminder that in spite of outstanding social services, improving programs for the elderly, and well-intentioned community development initiatives, many people in our culture are incredibly lonely.

It was a painful reminder that in spite of outstanding social services, improving programs for the elderly, and well-intentioned community development initiatives, many people in our culture are incredibly lonely. Stec wasn't lacking information; he died with newspapers by his side. Stec was lacking meaningful relationships. You might say that he was suffering from "Information Isolation."

INFORMATION ISOLATION

One reason we suffer from Information Isolation is our pursuit of self-sufficiency. We can access almost any information we need via the internet without leaving the safety of our home. Via email or cell phone, we can contact anyone, anywhere, anytime, without setting foot outside our door. With delivery systems such as Peapod for groceries and FedEx for everything from books to bikes, we can buy anything we want and have it placed on our front step. Not only do we no longer have to go to a movie theater to see a show, we don't even have to go to the video store. With Netflix, we can order whatever movie we want when we want it. And should we choose the daring task of actually leaving the house and risking the possibility of human contact, our attached garages allow us to drive away without having to make eye contact with our next-door neighbors.

Unfortunately, Information Isolation isn't relegated only to our neighborhoods. This kind of isolation is what too many of us experience week after week in our churches. It might not be a neighbor whose body is decaying while we sleep just yards away, but it might be the person we sit next to week after week whose soul is wasting away because he has bought the lie that following Christ is a "God and me" thing. Sure, he shows up week after week to celebrate and receive all sorts of good information, but he never has the privilege of experiencing life change through genuine biblical community.

Randy Frazee, in *Making Room for Life*, says, "It's possible to be in the company of others and still feel isolated. Community specialists call this brand of isolation experienced by the majority of Americans as 'crowded loneliness.' It is the most dangerous loneliness of all because it emits a false air of community that prevents us from diagnosing our dilemma correctly. We have exposure to people (and lots of valuable content), but not a deep connection to people."[2] And before you accuse me of being self-righteous, let me say that yes, this happens in my church too.

> It might not be a neighbor whose body is decaying while we sleep just yards away, but it might be the person we sit next to week after week whose soul is wasting away because he has bought the lie that following Christ is a "God and me" thing.

GOD'S BIG IDEA

Jesus offers us a solution to Information Isolation. One day a man who was considered a religious expert asked Jesus, "What is the most important commandment?" It seems like a good question for anyone to ask, but behind this man's question is some important background that we need to understand.

In Jesus' day, people had boiled the Bible down to 613 commandments, 613 rules. And everyone was told, "You have to keep these 613 commandments to be okay with God." One of the ways people tried to deal with these 613 commands was by dividing them into more important and less important commandments. Naturally, some controversy arose over which ones were more important and which ones were less important. So the religious expert was saying, "Help me out here — cut through this information overload and tell me which is *the* most important commandment. Remembering 613 rules doesn't work for me; figuring out more important and less important ones doesn't work for me. Just tell me the one that is most important." He was asking Jesus, "What's the Big Idea?" This man had loads of information, but information alone wasn't what he needed.

Jesus responded by giving him the Big Idea of all big ideas: "The most important one ... is this: ... 'Love the Lord your God with all your heart and with all your soul and with all your mind and with all your strength.' In the same breath Jesus added, "The second is this: 'Love your neighbor as yourself.' There is no commandment greater than these" (Mark 12:29 – 31). Now, notice something here. The man didn't ask, "What are the *two* most important commandments?" He asked for the single most important one. Jesus added the second one without being asked.

Why did he do that? I think Jesus didn't stop with "Love God with all you have" because he knew that many people had been taught a "just God and me" spirituality. In fact, many people in our day have been taught the same thing. I was brought up believing that all we really need is God: people are important, people matter, but what matters most is our personal relationship with God. Does that sound familiar? There was even a song about it. I grew up in a church that loved gospel music, and one song that was popular back then was called "On the Jericho Road." It went like this: "On the Jericho Road, there's room for just two. No more and no less, just Jesus and you."

Jesus added the second command so that we wouldn't fall into the "just Jesus and me" pattern of thinking that can lead to Information Isolation. When Jesus said, in essence, "Don't just love God; love other people with the same focus and energy with which you love yourself," he wasn't just talking about ethics and the importance of being good to other people. He was echoing God's original dream from the story of creation in Genesis. Jesus wants us to love our neighbors as ourselves not because that's what good Christian people should do but rather because that's how we are designed, how we are hardwired to live. Keeping both of these great commandments — to love God and to love others — is what it means to be a Christ follower.

> Jesus wants us to love our neighbors as ourselves not because that's what good Christian people should do but rather because that's how we are designed, how we are hardwired to live.

SMALL GROUPS

At Community Christian Church, we have three expectations of anyone who chooses to follow Jesus. We expect every person to celebrate, connect, and contribute weekly:

- When we *celebrate*, we focus primarily on our relationship with God. We can consistently celebrate the goodness of God through worship, Bible reading, prayer, meditation, and journaling.

- When we *connect*, we focus primarily on our relationship with God's family, the church. Our small groups are the best place for people to live out Jesus' Big Idea to love both God and others.
- When we *contribute*, we focus primarily on our relationship with the world. We can contribute weekly to God's work using our unique talents, passions, and resources.

At CCC, we launched small groups before we ever had a weekend celebration service. Experiencing biblical community through small groups is our antidote to Information Isolation. Small groups provide not only an environment where all three of these experiences can occur but also the encouragement and accountability any Christ follower needs to be what we call a growing "3C Christ follower."

Our small groups are the environment in which people experience the most dramatic life transformation. Here's one example:

> Experiencing biblical community through small groups is our antidote to Information Isolation.

Patty was the first to recognize a need for something more; she identified it as a spiritual issue. Her husband, Ralph, says that he just felt that life was very superficial — that too often, nothing really seemed to matter.

About that time a friend invited them to a weekend service at CCC. They admit it was different for them. They had some of the same questions many people have when they first come to CCC: "Where are the candles? Stained glass? Robes? Kneelers?" However, they experienced something unique in the service: energy, excitement, enthusiasm, a real *celebration* where people were actually happy to be there.

It wasn't long before they realized they wanted something more. They heard over and over again that a small group is a great place to connect with other people who are trying to get closer to God, but they were reluctant to give it a try. They could only imagine a bunch of "holy rollers." What they found was something quite different: friendship, encouragement, support, and a real *connection*. They met people they could count on, pray with, and have fun with. Ralph says, "My fears subsided when I learned I wouldn't have to stick my hand into a basket of snakes or sing 'Kum Ba Yah.'" After several months in the group, Ralph and Patty "went public" — they were baptized by their small group leader, John.

After that, Ralph and Patty say their spiritual journey kicked into high gear. They attended a LifeMap course, in which they began to understand the way God had uniquely created them to make a difference in the world. And for the first time they realized that God had given them gifts and passions that could be used to *contribute* to the cause of helping people find their way back to God. After working alongside his small group leader for a while, Ralph stepped up to lead a small group himself, and soon Patty began serving in Kids' City, the children's ministry at CCC.

Celebrate, connect, contribute. It's no accident that Ralph and Patty have experienced significant life transformation. They are experiencing God's dream for every one of us. In *Community 101*, Gilbert Bilezikian writes, "It is in small groups that people can get close enough to know each other, to care and share, to challenge and support, to confide and confess, to forgive and be forgiven, to laugh and weep together, to be accountable to each other, to watch over each other, and to grow together. Personal growth does not happen in isolation. It is the result of interactive relationships. Small groups

> Celebrate, connect, contribute. It's no accident that Ralph and Patty have experienced significant life transformation. They are experiencing God's dream for every one of us.

are God's gift to foster change in character and spiritual growth."[3] We have found that using the Big Idea in our small groups greatly increases the likelihood that our groups will become transforming communities.

BIG IDEA AND SMALL GROUPS: A TRANSFORMING COMBINATION

One of the people who influenced the development of small groups at CCC is Lyman Coleman, founder of Serendipity Publishing and a pioneer of the contemporary small group movement. Lyman has an unwavering passion for the church and has worked tirelessly and sacrificed much to train pastors and small group leaders. He speaks fondly of his experience in small groups through the 1950s, '60s, '70s, and '80s. He says that in each of these decades the church made great attempts to develop small groups but had a tendency to over-emphasize particular aspects of group life at the expense of others.

Lyman says that most small groups in the 1950s were almost exclusively about Bible study, "the deeper the better." Relationships were an afterthought if a thought at all. In the 1960s, not surprisingly, small groups reflected the culture of our day and took a turn toward activism; consequently, Bible study took a backseat. Relationships often were forged around a particular cause, but the cause wasn't necessarily biblical. Then in the 1970s small groups ushered in the era of "naval gazing," and both Bible study and activism took a backseat to self-reflection and personal growth.

Lyman's vision for the twenty-first century was that small groups would finally achieve a balance of three things: Bible study, relationships, and service. He called it the "three-legged stool" model. Take away one leg of a three-legged stool, and it will fall. Take away one of these three things from a small group, and it will fail. I've always thought that Lyman's historical take on small groups is very helpful for avoiding some common pitfalls; namely, too much focus on information and too little focus on transformation and life change.

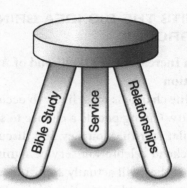

In the 1980s, Lyman proposed an idea that he called "pulpit groups" — small groups that would base their Bible studies or discussions on the sermon from the previous weekend service. At the time, only a few churches across the country were implementing this model. Lyman was convinced that this approach to small groups would have several benefits:

1. It would make it easier for a person with minimal Bible knowledge to lead a small group.
2. It would result in greater life transformation.
3. It would thematically tie in the theme of the weekend service with the small group experience during the week.

Lyman was a huge advocate of including nonbelievers and believers in the same small group and challenged people to place an empty chair in each group as a reminder of the "prodigals" who had yet to find their way back to God. He thought that featuring the same topic in both the weekend service and the small group would be an easy way to invite newcomers in a small group to a weekend celebration service. He never called this strategy the Big Idea, but in retrospect, I'd say it was very much the same idea. While not all of our small groups use the Big Idea in their weekly gatherings, more and more are starting to use it, and we are seeing a number of benefits as a result.

FIVE BENEFITS THE BIG IDEA BRINGS TO SMALL GROUPS

1. The Big Idea Increases the Likelihood of Application and Transformation

We believe that life change is most likely to occur within the context of community. Giving people a chance to sit in a circle with others on a similar spiritual journey and discuss the content of the previous weekend celebration service significantly increases the likelihood that they will actually apply the topic to their lives. Even the most dynamic and interactive celebration services tend to be primarily didactic: we talk, we sing, we dance, they listen, they watch. Small groups by nature are experiential and discussion oriented and, as a result, more likely to foster life change. In addition, because the topic of the discussion guide is tied directly to the topic of the weekend celebration service, every weekend our campus pastors and teaching team have a great opportunity to invite people to explore the topic further in a small group.

> Small groups by nature are experiential and discussion oriented and, as a result, more likely to foster life change.

2. The Big Idea Diminishes People's Fears of Leading a Small Group

One of the greatest challenges in launching new groups and keeping existing groups healthy and growing is identifying and recruiting potential small group leaders. We have found that the most common fears among potential small group leaders are the following:

"I don't know enough about the Bible."
"I don't have enough time to be a good leader."
"I've never thought of myself as a leader."

The weekend prior to the launch of every Big Idea series, we publish a small group discussion guide with a small group lesson that parallels each week's topic in that Big Idea series. Developing these discussion guides and making them available to our leaders significantly reduces their insecurities regarding leading. The Bible verses for discussion are included in the discussion guide, and the lessons require minimal preparation with helpful insights and directions for the leaders. (See the appendix for a link to a sample Big Idea small group discussion guide.)

3. The Big Idea Eliminates the Question, "What Do We Study Next?"

Small groups tend to become overly focused on the topic of their discussion, often at the expense of developing relationships and experiencing genuine biblical community. The relational small group experience can easily slip into more of a classroom teacher/student context. Anyone who has ever been part of a small group has spent more than a few sessions trying to answer the question, "What do we study next?" Recently I was told of a small group leader who spent hours researching possible topics for future study. On the evening he presented his ideas, someone in the group brought a new book he had been reading and in a matter of minutes hijacked the conversation. The leader's research was forgotten, and the group was swayed by this persuasive member to "vote" for his suggestion. The group member meant no harm, but who do you think knew more about what the group needed? And what are the chances that the leader will put so much time and effort into researching future topics? Sticking to the Big Idea minimizes this challenge and offers small groups an easy plan to follow when it comes to subject matter.

> Small groups tend to become overly focused on the topic of their discussion, often at the expense of developing relationships and experiencing genuine biblical community.

4. The Big Idea Provides Another Avenue to Communicate Vision

Our small group directors collaborate with the leader of our teaching team to write the small group discussion guides. Since these directors are responsible for the overall health and direction of the small group ministry, they have a great opportunity to provide vision and direction for the small groups through the content of these guides. While we consistently communicate vision through our monthly Leadership Community gathering, weekend celebration services, e-communications, and so on, the content of these guides gives us one more vehicle through which to communicate to our leaders and small group members.

5. The Big Idea Increases the Quality of Small Group Experiences

Small groups are a risk! They are a low-control venture and by nature are a decentralized way to pastor and care for people. We want to do whatever we can to make our leaders as successful as possible. With the proliferation of small group discussion guides (both good and bad) and an array of other uncontrollable variables, the quality of any given small group experience will be uncertain. Even with a well-trained leader, a small group can easily be derailed by choosing content that is less than stimulating or by selecting a discussion guide that does not foster life-changing conversations. While many factors contribute to a great small group experience, writing our own curriculum or discussion guides increases the likelihood that each group will have an outstanding small group experience.

We have found the Big Idea to be very effective in helping our small groups to become places of real life change and transformation, not simply places where people can gather more and more information.

It's too late for Adolf Stec of Chicago, but our hope is that his tragic life and death will serve as a constant reminder that people all around us are suffering from Information Isolation. They have access to loads of data with the touch of a finger, yet at the end of the day (or at the end of their lives), all of that data might ultimately do them no good at all. However, as a community of faith, we can help people combine that information with life-changing relationships in small groups, and they can experience true transformation.

> We have found the Big Idea to be very effective in helping our small groups to become places of real life change and transformation, not simply places where people can gather more and more information.

Here's how Kathy Fuhrman, also from the Chicago area, describes her experience leading a small group with the Big Idea:

SMALL GROUP AND THE BIG IDEA

Our small group has used the Big Idea discussion guides for more than a year now. One of the things we like about the Big Idea is that it gives us the opportunity to discuss the weekend message in more detail. As a result, we find that we're more likely to apply the principles of the Big Idea to our lives. We often spend some time reviewing the service at the beginning of our discussion. It gives people the opportunity to raise questions from the message or discuss a significant moment from the service. As a leader, I like it because the service has helped me better prepare for the group discussion.

Several months ago our weekend series was titled New Year's Revolutions, and the topic for the week was "Relational Revolutionary." The session concluded with a challenge for the group to do a service project together. At the same time some of us in the group were following the diary of Ben and Melody, a couple in our church who started a mission in Rwanda. They were hosting a refugee family from Africa and the diary chronicled their experience. We wanted to help them and decided to invite them to come to our group and talk about Global Family Rescue and their work in Rwanda.

Their presentation touched our hearts. They left us with some pictures of the fatherless families they were hoping to help. Over the next few weeks, we discussed this as a group. Three of the couples in our group decided to help one family together. For one of the couples, this was the first time that they had given beyond a tithe. They spent some significant time discussing this new direction for their lives. I was very excited to see them take this step in their spiritual journey.

A few months into our sponsorship, we received word that the widow we were sponsoring was avoiding meetings with the caseworker and there were rumors of her spending some of the money on alcohol. Ben emailed us and told us that the board had put her on three months' probation and that had ended without resolution of the problem. "What would you like to do?" they asked us. We could drop her sponsorship and pick up someone else. They would continue to work with Marie, provide accountability, and eventually offer sponsorship to her again.

At our next small group, we sat around the dining room table discussing our options. We truly felt the enormity of the situation. I still am moved with emotions when I remember our faces around that table discussing the real-life decisions involving forgiveness, restitution, discipline, honoring God with our money, bearing others' burdens, and trying to feel someone else's pain. Later that week I received an email from her caseworker. He asked us to give Marie more time and renewed his commitment to continue to try to reach out to her. He also let us know that he had a pastor who was willing to try to reach her as well.

In the end we decided to give her some more time and continue to send our support. We tried to imagine what she had gone through in staying alive through the genocide and trying to keep her family alive. We tried to imagine the things that she was trying to forget by drinking. We committed to pray for her more than ever.

Just last month we received an email picture of our Marie. She is smiling and holding the card and photos that we sent to her. She continues to meet with the caseworker and the pastor. She is working through her drinking problem. We sent extra money for her to buy two goats.

When we first made this decision to support one family together, I was concerned about making it work. It's difficult to be involved with other people's money. But after experiencing that group discussion, I knew that God had a plan — that doing this as a group caused us to talk about what we are doing with our money. It gave us an incredible opportunity to be real with each other. Our lives have been changed. My life has been changed.

God used our small group and the Big Idea to impact not only the life of a widow in Africa but the lives of my small group in Naperville, Illinois. I am grateful for these significant moments in life when God gives us a glimpse of himself and we get just a peek into heaven.

CHAPTER 3

CREATING MISSIONAL VELOCITY

When we started Community Christian Church, the membership included my brother, Jon, and me and three friends from college. We didn't have a facility. We didn't have any people. And we didn't have any sense! The one thing we all had was a passion to help people find their way back to God. And that simple phrase became our mission: "helping people find their way back to God." During the first eight years, one by one people began to align themselves with our stated mission until the church grew to encompass about eight hundred people who were passionate about helping people find their way back to God. Over the next eight years, through circumstances only God could have made possible, we became a multisite church and our mission began to pick up velocity. During that time we transitioned from being one church with eight hundred people meeting in two services at one location to being one church with five thousand people meeting in twenty-plus services at eight locations all over Chicagoland.

The velocity began to build up as we started a network of new churches called the NewThing Network (www.newthing.org). Thirty-five people moved from Chicago to Denver to help start a new church. Another fifteen people moved to Southern California to plant a new church. Still more people moved to Detroit to start another missional church. One group moved to the heart of New

> The velocity began to build up as we started a network of new churches called the NewThing Network (www.newthing.org).

York City, relocating from Chicago to Manhattan. And still others moved from Chicago to Boston to accomplish the mission of Jesus. And if you were here, you could literally feel the missional velocity! So how did we come to experience this kind of velocity?

EDUCATED BEYOND OBEDIENCE

I was doing an internship in Southern California and was just about to graduate from Bible college when I heard Juan Carlos Ortiz make this statement: "The average Christian is educated to at least three years beyond their level of obedience." Instantly I knew it was true of me, and I had a hunch it was true about much of the church. Ortiz went on to explain that there were times when he would preach only a handful of sermons to his congregation over the course of a year. He would show up and teach the same Big Idea week after week after week until the people began to put it into action. So every week those who attended one of the largest churches in all of Argentina would hear the exact same teaching until they began, as Ortiz called it, "living the Word."

Ortiz tells the story of how this practice first began after a very energetic and stirring Sunday worship service. The voices of the people rang with the enthusiastic vigor that is so characteristic of Pentecostal churches. The prayers were issued with a tone of charismatic fervor. And the people felt sure the Spirit of God was there as Pastor Ortiz came to deliver the teaching. The text for the week was right out of the lectionary passage. During the week Ortiz had prepared a message to remind the congregation of the importance of loving one another. He had spent a great deal of time praying over the message, studying, and carefully recording his thoughts. He believed that God had truly guided him as he prepared each point and selected each illustration, and thus he approached the pulpit with boldness. But then something happened about halfway between his seat and the pulpit. He heard a voice.

"Juan."

"Yes, Lord."

"How many times have you preached on this passage in this church?"

"I don't know — maybe a dozen."

As he was about to step into the pulpit and speak, he heard the same voice ask, "Did any of those sermons do any good?"

Maybe you can sympathize with Ortiz's dilemma: a minister stands before the congregation and suddenly realizes that he or she has the wrong message. In that moment the minister knows that the words that seemed inspired on Tuesday are going to sound like clanging gongs on Sunday.

Ortiz stood still, frozen in time. All thoughts evaporated from his mind. He looked over the congregation and saw the people he had led to Christ. He saw people he had counseled during times of emotional turmoil, as well as people he had visited in the hospital at 2:00 a.m. as their loved ones clung to life. He saw people who had heard the Christian message taught over and over again, in Sunday school lessons, small group Bible studies, and his own sermons; they knew the words but still struggled to live out the message. Finally, he said, "Love one another." Then he walked back to his seat and sat down.

The people sat in motionless silence. This Pentecostal congregation that could handle fiery preaching and passionate praise didn't know what to do with utter stillness. Then Pastor Ortiz stood up, walked to the pulpit again, and said, "Love one another." As he returned to his seat once more, heads began to turn from side to side. People looked at one another with questioning eyes, silently asking, "What should we do now?" Eyebrows rose. Shoulders shrugged. Bewilderment settled on everyone's face. After waiting a few minutes, Ortiz walked to the pulpit one more time.

He positioned himself and then very deliberately said, "Love one another," then returned to his seat once again.

After a few moments a man stood up and said, "Brothers and sisters, I think I understand what Pastor Ortiz is talking about. He is asking me to love you." Then he pointed to a family seated next to him and asked, "But how can I love you when I do not even know your name?" The man proceeded to introduce himself to the family and ask them questions in the hope of discovering ways in which he could express his love.

Another man stood up and said, "I also understand what Pastor Ortiz is saying. He wants me to love Carlos [a man sitting three pews in front of him], but how can I love Carlos when I still hold a grudge against him?" The man left his pew and approached Carlos to apologize, and the two were reconciled. With this, the floodgates were opened. People stood up and began to circulate, asking what they could do for one another.

That Sunday amazing things happened. A husband and wife had come to the city seeking medical treatment for their little girl, and they didn't have enough money to return home; someone purchased bus tickets for them. Another young man who was looking for a job was introduced to a man who owned a business and needed an extra worker; the young man got a job. While all of these displays of love were taking place, Ortiz remained seated, praying and watching one of the most powerful sermons ever delivered in that church. The congregation was never the same after that worship service.

Ortiz was using the Big Idea. What you see and hear in this story is what the Big Idea does best: it puts the focus on the mission and others and takes the focus off of information and me. How many times have you heard someone say, "I just really need something deeper"? You probably think to yourself, "If it gets any deeper in here, we may drown in it!" Or maybe you try to take the comment seriously, but you know this person isn't involved in a small group or in regular serving opportunities, and you doubt he or she has tithed even once! I wish I could say that the Big Idea eliminates people's delusion that what they really need is something "deeper." But because of the repetitive teaching and the insistence on application, the focus is much more on the mission of Jesus and service to others than on ways we can increase people's personal Christian database.

After seeing his sermon "in action" that Sunday, Ortiz determined he would never again teach a message that was not going to be lived out to accomplish the mission of Jesus. And if that meant preaching only five or six sermons a year, that's what he would do. He would teach one Big Idea and insist that it be missionally applied and lived out. He was determined that his church would be not a place of information but a place of transformation that would produce missional velocity.

> He was determined that his church would be not a place of information but a place of transformation that would produce missional velocity.

Missional velocity? Yep. Juan Carlos Ortiz never used that phrase, but it's exactly what he was looking for. Erwin McManus, in *An Unstoppable Force*, does a great job of describing this velocity and the way that movements occur. Stick with me on this; I think it will help. He starts by reminding us that the scientific formula for momentum is mass multiplied by velocity:

MOVEMENT = MASS × MISSIONAL VELOCITY

Erwin goes on to tell us that mass without velocity has no impact because it is stationary. Velocity without mass is motion without the ability to have an impact. If we view the church as a movement that is to have an impact, there must be momentum — and that requires missional velocity. Ortiz had the mass; he was pastoring one of the largest churches in Argentina. Now he just needed to get it moving in the right direction. What he wanted, and what the Big Idea gave his church (and will give your church), is missional velocity.

For most of us reading this book and contemplating this topic, mass is not a problem. I would contend that if you have a small group of twelve, you have enough mass to make an impact, and that impact could gain momentum and become a movement. Jesus proved it. He stood before each of his disciples and laid out the Big Idea with a clear call for action: "Follow me" (Matt. 4:19). In time, he explained the next Big Idea in the form of the two greatest commandments: "Love God" and "Love others" (see Matt. 22:37 – 39). Just before Jesus left this planet, he stood before his small group for the very last time and said, "Okay, let me give you one more Big Idea." Then he told them, "You will receive power when the Holy Spirit comes on you; and you will be my witnesses in Jerusalem, and in all Judea and Samaria, and to the ends of the earth" (Acts 1:8). The direction of the Big Idea was what gave the mass a missional velocity and brought about a movement that turned the world upside down!

> The direction of the Big Idea was what gave the mass a missional velocity and brought about a movement that turned the world upside down!

Velocity is defined as "speed with direction." You need to have both speed and direction in order to have missional velocity.

MISSIONAL VELOCITY = SPEED WITH DIRECTION

You can have speed, but if it's not headed in a particular direction, you can't harness it to create momentum. It's very possible to be moving at an extremely fast pace but merely be moving back and forth. Along with speed, you need a definite direction. When you put speed and direction together, you have velocity. And when a church combines the clear direction of the Big Idea with the speedy obedience of the Big Idea application, it has missional velocity. Let's take a look at how to create missional velocity by starting with directional alignment and then discussing speedy obedience.

THE BIG IDEA = DIRECTIONAL ALIGNMENT

For the first eight years of Community Christian Church, we were one church meeting in one location — like most churches! And like most churches, every Sunday for eight years we had one message delivered by one teaching pastor, one band led by one worship leader, and one children's ministry directed by one set of leaders. One of everything! But then we became one church with two locations — and everything changed. Now we needed two teaching pastors, two bands, two worship leaders, two sets of Kids' City leaders. Two of everything! Like never before we had to recruit and develop leaders and artists. The task was daunting, but its necessity was obvious.

What was not so obvious was the question of alignment. If we were to move forward as one church at two sites, how could we

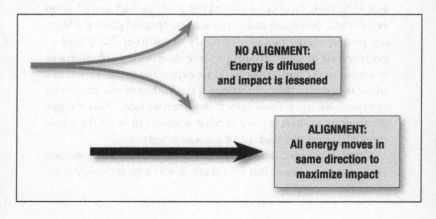

NO ALIGNMENT:
Energy is diffused
and impact is lessened

ALIGNMENT:
All energy moves in
same direction to
maximize impact

make sure that we would maximize our missional impact and not merely diffuse our energy in two different directions?

The question of alignment is often overlooked by growing churches because they simply grow larger at one site. Consequently, they still need only one teaching pastor, one band and one worship leader, and one set of children's ministry leaders. Single-site churches can maintain the illusion of alignment longer than multisite churches can, but one day they get a wake-up call to the fact that dozens of people are on staff, hundreds or thousands of people are showing up, and everyone is headed in a different direction. Bill Hybels describes that experience at Willow Creek:

> I wish I could say that this staff alignment came off as smoothly as the jibes after our crew practice, but it just didn't happen like that. Some staff who had operated with enormous independence for a decade or more weren't too excited about having to modify their sub-ministry plans in order to put more energy into the wider church challenge. Some felt we were changing the rules in the middle of the game, and, in a way, we were.
>
> For many years we had hired staff, given them a budget, and said, "Go build a single-adult ministry, build a youth ministry, and build a music ministry. Have fun." And they were having a ball. But some of them were headed in dramatically different directions from the church at large. While they were all engaged in worthwhile endeavors, they were not all consistently moving the people in their ministries toward the goals we had agreed upon as a church. Some sub-ministries had no specific plans for helping people engage more consistently in spiritual disciplines or get involved in small groups or serve as ministry volunteers or reach out to the poor. How could we expect the congregation as a whole to move in those directions if the leaders of sub-ministries were not holding up those values? But when we said, "Now it's time for all of us to share a piece of what it means to build the whole church," some cried foul, and it got a little ugly.
>
> Most of the staff were receptive and jumped on board as soon as they saw the issue. But for others, it was a long bumpy road,

longer and bumpier than I ever anticipated. It took many months filled with meetings and discussions to help everybody see that a federation of sub-ministries was neither biblical nor sustainable.[1]

The question of direction and alignment hit us right in the face when we made the move from becoming one church that met only in Naperville to becoming one church that met in both Naperville and Romeoville. One of the most

> Single-site churches can maintain the illusion of alignment longer than multisite churches can, but one day they get a wake-up call to the fact that dozens of people are on staff, hundreds or thousands of people are showing up, and everyone is headed in a different direction.

significant decisions we had to make concerned the teaching themes for celebration services. Here are some of the questions that came up: "Should both sites use the same themes? Should we have one site a week behind the other and rotate bands, worship leaders, and other creative teams? Should each site develop its own themes and artists?"

After much discussion and debate, we made the decision to have both locations use the same teaching themes. But that only brought on another wave of questions and what-ifs: "What if all of the large groups (children, students, adults, etc.) worked off of the same themes and we customized those themes for each age group?" "What if our Kids' City small groups experienced the same themes as the adults? Then families could have significant spiritual conversations about what they experienced at church, knowing that every family member was focused on the same topic." "What if we had one huge creative brainstorming meeting every week with the artistic leaders from every ministry—everyone working together to develop ideas for all of our services?" "What if we created a teaching team so that the teaching pastors collaborated on every mes-

> Families could have significant spiritual conversations about what they experienced at church, knowing that every family member was focused on the same topic.

sage and actually created the manuscript together, making it the best they could and then teaching it at the various sites?"

I know it would make a better story to tell you that the church underwent a major upheaval during this transition phase, but that really isn't what happened. In one of the quickest turnarounds I've ever seen — just a few months after going multisite — we implemented the amazing process we now call the Big Idea. So every week at Community Christian Church, one Big Idea is taught and experienced in all large groups and small groups and comes to life through families in their homes.

In retrospect, the move to one Big Idea was vitally important for us at the time when we added a second location. But it is even more important now that we have eight sites locally and five sites nationally, because the Big Idea provides directional alignment among all of our ministries and sites, as well as a stronger focus on our mission — helping people find their way back to God.

Here is how the Big Idea was executed just a few months ago. Remember back in chapter 1 the email I received from a mom whose little boys emptied their banks and gave away every

U GOT GAME

penny to help families in Rwanda? It all started with a Big Idea series that challenged people to reach a new level of serving and contribut-

ing to Jesus' mission. We came up with an athletic metaphor; below is the graphic we used for the Kids' City and Student Community ministries:

And here is the graphic we used for all of our adult celebration services:

The Big Idea gets everyone of every age aligned and moving in the same direction.

The Big Idea Moves the Whole Family in the Same Direction

Having all of our kids elementary age and older experience the same Big Idea as the adults creates alignment at home and increases the likelihood that families will engage in spiritual conversations. It also allows parents to enter into spiritual conversations with more confidence since they just spent an hour learning about the same Big Idea as their children. And when kids give their parents a Big Idea family page with ideas for family activities and discussions, the stage is set for missional velocity to pick up at home.

The Big Idea Moves All Small Groups in the Same Direction

The Big Idea that people experience in the weekend celebration service is the same Big Idea that they will experience during the week in their small group. As a result, small group members come more prepared for the conversation, with a greater possibility that God's Spirit is already working on them in this area of their lives. The alignment between the large group experience and the small group experience creates the powerful force called missional velocity.

The Big Idea Moves All Ministries in the Same Direction

If each of our ministries (adults', students', and children's) had a different experience and each of our eight locations had a different experience, the effect would be like that of shot fired from a shotgun. But since every ministry and every site experiences the same Big Idea, the effect is like that of a single bullet. With shot, you may hit more area, but you diffuse the impact. With a bullet, you have much greater impact. If we send people home with a lot of little ideas, we diffuse the energy; but with the Big Idea, we create missional velocity and maximize the impact!

The Big Idea Moves All Campuses and Sites in the Same Direction

Legendary church consultant Lyle Schaller made this prediction about multisite churches: "There will be many churches that will have two sites, almost none with three sites, and a whole bunch more that will have four or more sites." When we asked him to explain, he said the difference will have a lot to do with alignment.

Directional alignment involves making sure that all of our energy is moving in the same direction.

We do several things to maintain directional alignment as a multisite church. For example, we have the "Four Ones": one vision, one staff, one budget, and one eldership. Leadership Community, our monthly gathering of all of the leaders from every ministry at every location, helps us realign each month. But on a week-to-week basis, the one thing that creates alignment so that all of our sites are moving in the same direction is the Big Idea. Perhaps more than anything else it is what produces missional velocity.

The Big Idea Moves the Whole Network in the Same Direction

Every week a network of like-minded churches all across the country collaborate to create and experience the same Big Idea. Churches in Chicago, Denver, Detroit, Manhattan, and Boston are all moving forward in their large group worship services and small group communities with the Big Idea. This alignment of focus and energy generates an unmistakable velocity for the mission of Jesus.

BIG IDEA = SPEEDY OBEDIENCE

For a Christian, as we described in chapter 1, the expectation is simply church attendance. But for a Christ follower, the measure of maturity is determined by the speed of obedience. The most mature Christ follower is not the person who has attended the most church events or accumulated the most information about Jesus, but rather the person whose heart is most transformed. And transformation is seen when a person hears God and responds with swift obedience. The repetitiveness of the Big Idea and the emphasis on putting into action what we learn combine to bring about speedy obedience.

When I think of speedy obedience, I think about John, a man who began following Jesus at Community Christian Church and in a matter of months not only became a leader and then a coach of leaders but also quit his high-paying job to join the church-planting team headed for Denver. That is speedy obedience. Or I think of Shawna, who also in a matter of months was baptized as a new believer and quickly moved into leadership; when she felt God was leading her to join a team planting a church in Manhattan, she left her job and friends behind and obeyed. Or I think of Ellen, who was baptized into Christ on a Wednesday night and then showed up that Friday night at a leadership training event to become a small group leader. The Big Idea creates in Christ followers speedy obedience, which in turn creates missional velocity in the church.

PART TWO

• • • •

What's the Big Idea?

CHAPTER 4

THE GENIUS
OF THE "AND"

When Jim Collins coined the phrase "Genius of the And," he was explaining that truly great organizations are comfortable living within paradox. He put it this way:

> Visionary companies do not brutalize themselves with the "Tyranny of the Or" — the purely rational view that says you can have either A *or* B, but not both. They reject having to make a choice between stability *or* progress; cult-like cultures *or* individual autonomy; home-grown managers *or* fundamental change; conservative practices *or* Big Hairy Audacious Goals; making money *or* living according to values and purposes. Instead, they embrace the "Genius of the And" — the paradoxical view that allows them to pursue both A *and* B at the same time.[1]

God's dream for his church is also a greatness filled with paradox:

> The first will be last, and the last will be first.
> The greatest will be the least, and the least will be the greatest.
> The rich will become poor, and the poor will become rich.
> The weak will be strong, and the strong will be weak.
> Try to save your life, and you will lose it; lose your life, and you
>   will save it.
> What once was gain is now counted as loss.
> In losing this life, you gain life eternal.

As Christ followers, we should be comfortable living in the midst of paradox.

The Big Idea brings paradoxical benefits to the ministry of any church. Community Christian Church experiences at least a half dozen of these "genius of the And" benefits. Before I describe our top six benefits, let's start with the one benefit that transcends them all.

PARADOX: THE BIG IDEA IS LESS *AND* MORE

Barry Schwartz, in *The Paradox of Choice*, reminds us that the common thinking among social scientists is that added options can only make us better off as a society. The thinking is that those who care about the added options will benefit, and those who don't care can always ignore the added options. Sounds like it makes sense!

But a series of studies titled "When Choice Is De-motivating" provides evidence to the contrary. One fascinating study took place in a gourmet food store where researchers set up a sample table with exotic high-quality jams for customers to sample. Customers who sampled the jam would receive a dollar-off coupon if they chose to buy some. At first the researchers set out six varieties of jam for customers to taste; then they set out twenty-four varieties. In both cases, all twenty-four varieties were available and for sale. Here's what happened:

- The large variety of jams attracted the most people.
- The same number of people sampled the large variety of jams and the small variety of jams.
- Only 3 percent of the people who tasted the large variety of jams actually bought some, while 30 percent of the people who tasted the small variety of jams bought some.

Schwartz concludes, "Our culture sanctifies freedom of choice so profoundly that the benefits of infinite options seem self-evident ... too many alternatives can create a problem."[2]

Many churches are discovering the same thing when it comes to teaching — too many alternatives can create a problem, and the solution is the paradox of the Big Idea. One of those churches is North-Point Church in Alpharetta, Georgia. NorthPoint constantly stresses in its teaching ministry values such as "Teach less for more," "Narrow the focus," and "Concentrate on the irreducible minimums." The church has reached the same conclusion that we have: more is less — and less is more. More often results in less action, and less often results in more action. It's a paradox. What we are discovering is that offering people just one Big Idea at a time results in more action, not less. That action helps grow Christ followers and accomplish the mission of Jesus.

> Many churches are discovering the same thing when it comes to teaching — too many alternatives can create a problem, and the solution is the paradox of the Big Idea.

What are some of the other paradoxical benefits of the Big Idea? I'm glad you asked. Here they are, and they are best explained in terms of the Genius of the And.

1. ENERGY: LESS EFFORT *AND* BETTER STUFF

"They got the same work done nearly ten times as fast!"[3] This was one of Warren Bennis's observations in *Organizing Genius* regarding a group that experienced the power of creative collaboration. The Big Idea is a process designed for teamwork. Over and over again as a result of creative collaboration, we are seeing our teams and churches produce better stuff with less effort, resulting in greater stewardship of our energy.

Synergy of the Big Idea

Whenever we add a new church to our NewThing Network and it gets to experience the Big Idea process, it almost immediately feels the synergy. Dave Dummit, lead pastor at 2|42 Community, a NewThing Network church in Detroit, puts it this way: "I spend less time on message prep and get a better product. As a church planter, it frees me up to focus more time on leadership development and vision casting. And it's fun!" He is experiencing the synergy of collaborating on the Big Idea. Synergy is the interaction of two or more forces so that their combined effect is greater than the sum of their individual effects. When teaching pastors from five churches come together to create one message, the result is tremendous synergy. While most pastors will invest twenty to twenty-five hours of energy each week in crafting a message that will both teach and inspire their congregations, individual teachers using the Big Idea process will invest ten to twelve hours of energy each week and deliver a more challenging and inspiring message.

> Whenever we add a new church to our NewThing Network and it gets to experience the Big Idea process, it almost immediately feels the synergy.

Efficiency of the Big Idea

Several efficiencies emerge through the Big Idea collaborative process. Take, for example, the area of video production. Since we are working with four other churches to develop the Big Idea, when a truly great video idea comes up, there is no reason for all five churches to cast, film, edit, and produce that video. Instead, one of the churches will take the lead in creating that video product and all of us will share it.

You don't have to be part of a network of churches to experience these efficiencies. If two or three ministries (adults', students', and children's, for example) collaborate on a Big Idea, there will be times when the product you're creating for students will also work for kids. Other times the product you're creating for adults will also work for students. Occasionally you will come up with an idea that will work effectively for all ages. These efficiencies aren't forced but emerge as you work side by side in a collaborative environment to create one Big Idea.

For the last eight years I have seen this synergy and efficiency at work, and it is absolutely true that the Big Idea demands less effort and the result is better stuff. It is an energy saver!

2. INNOVATION: NEW IDEAS *AND* ALWAYS GOOD IDEAS

Every week through the Big Idea process we pull together a variety of teams from a variety of places to come up with brand-new and creative ideas. And these ideas are almost always good ones — though not always at first. In fact, we often come up with more bad ideas than good ones. But since the Big Idea process takes place within a healthy community that allows everyone to speak lovingly and honestly, only the good ideas make it as finished products. A tremendous benefit of the Big Idea is the opportunity to innovate and brainstorm freely, with confidence that the process will allow only the good ideas to survive.

Constant Brainstorming

Every Tuesday at 9:00 a.m. CST, the brainstorming begins in Chicago. It also begins in Denver at 8:00 a.m. RMT and in Detroit, Manhattan, and Boston at 10:00 a.m. EST. This is when the first of our meetings begins each week to plan the Big Idea nine weeks in advance. (See chapter 6, "Creating Your One-Year Big Idea Plan," for a timeline.) The rhythm and discipline of these meetings create a culture that fosters innovation. Peter Drucker, in *Innovation and Entrepreneurship*, explains how a culture of innovation is created: "Systematic innovation consists in the purposeful and organized search for changes."[4]

> The Big Idea process lends a purposeful and organized rhythm to our brainstorming.

The Big Idea process lends a purposeful and (sometimes) organized rhythm to our brainstorming. This culture cannot be contained within one meeting. The innovation oozes out into every other part of the church so that the brainstorming doesn't end when the meetings end. The brainstorming of new ideas continues in hallway conversations, cell phone calls, posts on blogs, lunch meetings, basketball games, and emails. The constant brainstorming is great — but it could also kill us. The barrage of new ideas along with our bent to "lead with a yes" could easily overwhelm us and overcommit us. Fortunately, the Big Idea process includes the built-in counterbalance of constant critiquing.

Constant Critiquing

In the same way that the Big Idea process inspires constant brainstorming, it also insists on constant critiquing. Five weeks after planning the Big Idea and four weeks before it is actually implemented, we reevaluate it and ask ourselves, "Can we really do this?" "Does all of this contribute to the Big Idea?" "Does any of this distract from the Big Idea?" "How are we doing at pulling this Big Idea together?"

Then at lunch on Wednesday after the weekend of the Big Idea, we step back and ask, "So how did we do?" This meeting includes a Zoomerang survey (www.zoomerang.com) that our staff members fill out online; the results come back to each of us looking like the chart on pages 70 and 71.

The survey is emailed to all of our staff and key leaders. We evaluate each of these categories in our Kids' City, Student Community, and adult ministries. The survey gives respondents the following choices on a 1 to 5 scale:

1	2	3	4	5
Poor–need to change immediately	Below expectations	Meets expectations	Exceeds expectations	Heaven on earth

As you can see in the survey of this particular weekend at Community Christian Church, some areas and locations exceeded our expectations (3 and above), while other areas failed to meet our expectations (below 3). To some, using this type of survey may seem critical and harsh; to us, it's an important part of creating a culture of innovation that fosters new ideas and good ideas.

The rhythm of these critiquing meetings and the value of collaboration create an environment where people are encouraged to express their ideas and criticism freely. If *criticism* is a bad word to you, think again. Patrick Lencioni, in *The Five Dysfunctions of a Team*, warns of the fear of conflict and of teams that are "incapable of engaging in unfiltered and passionate debate."[5] Isn't it much better to hear someone say, "That will never work!" on a Tuesday four weeks ahead of time than to suddenly become aware of it in front of a few hundred or thousand people during a church service?

> The rhythm of these critiquing meetings and the value of collaboration create an environment where people are encouraged to express their ideas and criticism freely.

The tug-of-war between brainstorming and critiquing gives us a healthy tension that allows us to innovate constantly with new ideas that are (almost) always good ideas.

	HomeTown Aurora	Montgomery Oswego	North downtown NNHS	North Yellow Box
The Big Idea	3.0	4.0	3.0	3.2
Effectiveness of "hptwbtG"	3.0	3.0	3.0	3.1
Moving people toward the 3Cs	3.0	4.0	3.0	3.6
Music	3.0	3.5	4.0	3.2
Production	3.0	3.5	2.0	2.9
Media	2.0	3.0	3.0	2.8
Theater (sketch)	3.0	4.0		3.2
Teaching	3.0	3.5	3.0	3.2
First Impressions	3.0	3.0	3.0	2.9
Next Steps (spiritual development)	3.0	3.0	3.0	3.0
Facility	3.0	4.0	3.0	3.0
Small group curriculum	3.0	4.0		3.0
Average	2.9	3.5	3.0	3.1
Number of respondents	2	2	1	11

Jon Ferguson	Great energy in the worship at Romeoville. Band did a nice job backing up the kids too. Loved the kid moment. It came off very nicely.
Scott Knollenberg	Great series. Good to see kids on stage and proud parents smiling and laughing in the crowd. Once again, it's a bit hard on Romeoville Campus when we do the kids' thing on stage so early in the service on Sundays.
Tim Bakker	Great service; loved having the kids involved. Service ended up being exceptionally long. KC video was very well done. Great short film for Saturday night. Had more significant challenges with greeting and direction for families in the CAC on Sunday morning.

Pilsen Chicago	Romeoville	Shorewood	Grand Total	Average
3.0	3.4	4.0	3.3	3.3
3.0	2.8	4.0	3.1	3.2
3.0	3.2	4.0	3.4	3.4
2.7	3.4	3.5	3.3	3.3
2.7	2.6	3.5	2.9	2.8
2.3	2.8	3.0	2.7	2.7
	3.5	4.0	3.4	3.5
3.0	3.2	3.0	3.2	3.1
3.3	3.0	3.0	3.0	3.0
3.0	3.0	3.0	3.0	3.0
3.3	3.0	4.0	3.2	3.3
3.0	3.0	3.0	3.2	3.1
2.9	3.1	3.5		
3	5	2		

Tony Germann	Media shout setup was not good: missing lyrics to songs; the audio track for Communion was only 2.5 minutes! Service went way too long: Kids' City moment — although awesome — went way beyond the allotted time in the Big Idea cue sheet. The Arts need to address some quality-control issues that have been problematic the last several weeks.
Lupe Kalter	Mary P. did an excellent job delivering the importance of the 3Cs. Kelly R. did her part leading worship in the adults' service Kids' City style. John C. popped his buttons off his shirt showing his T-shirt — "I'm in."
Vicki Thompson	It was great having the kids in the large group! Very fun! The video was pretty jumpy at the beginning of Dave's talk. It smoothed out and was fine for the rest of the teaching time.

3. TARGET GENERATIONS: BOOMERS, BUSTERS, *AND* MOSAICS

The Big Idea process transcends generational differences and appeals to all. Boomers (born between 1946 and 1964), Busters (born between 1965 and 1983), and Mosaics (born between 1984 and 2002) — no matter what your generation, the Big Idea process offers both an experiential and a propositional truth.

Let's examine the Big Idea through the lens of modernity and postmodernity. Moderns want a step-by-step plan for how to do it; postmoderns need an experience with God. Moderns want cognitive content with clear instructions for spiritual development; postmoderns want a community that will help guide them on their spiritual journey. Moderns want a strong emphasis on propositional truth; postmoderns want something relational that they can feel. How can you accomplish the "Genius of the And"?

Postmoderns Love It

The Big Idea process appeals to the postmodern mind because every Big Idea is a new and unique experience in which people have a chance to respond to God's prompting. The Big Idea is more than just cognitive content and an intellectual idea; it is a gathering (sometimes in small groups and sometimes in large groups) that helps people encounter the living God. Big Idea experiences are best facilitated in a community in which postmoderns can discover where God is moving and follow.

> The Big Idea process appeals to the postmodern mind because every Big Idea is a new and unique experience in which people have a chance to respond to God's prompting.

Moderns Love It Too!

The Big Idea also appeals to the modern mindset, because each week every gathering includes a clear application of what to do next and how to take the next step. The Big Idea can always be summarized in a paragraph that gives moderns the cognitive content they want. The Big Idea provides moderns with the security of being grounded in the propositional truth of Scripture.

The Big Idea has the unique ability to be both linear and experiential, both propositional and relational, both personal and communal — the genius of the And.

4. CURRICULUM: TARGETED *AND* REPRODUCIBLE

The Big Idea is more than a curriculum; it is a process for creating God experiences for anyone in any place. The Big Idea is a tool that allows you to create a curriculum that is targeted to any age or any setting and that at the same time is highly reproducible.

The Big Idea Works Right Here!

Every week at Community Christian Church, we have one Big Idea that gets translated into the language of kids, the language of students, and the language of adults. The same Big Idea is effectively applied to each of these target populations. Recently we did a series on family relationships. The kids' theme was a takeoff from the movie *Incredibles*, and we called it "Incredible Families." At the same time, the series for Student Community was titled "The Family Survival Guide," and the series for adults was titled "Parental Guidance Required." We targeted the same Big Idea to three different age groups. The graphics we used appear on the following page.

The Big Idea Works There Too!

The Big Idea doesn't end with one location; it is highly reproducible. When Community Christian Church went multisite eight years ago, we reproduced the Big Idea at another CCC location. We have continued to reproduce the Big Idea, and it is now used at eight CCC locations. At our eighth site, we translate the Big Idea into Spanish!

Four years ago, when a group of thirty-five people moved from Chicago to Denver to start a new church, we reproduced the Big Idea for a suburban Denver church, Jacob's Well Community Church. Since that time we have seen the Big Idea used effectively in rural Midwest settings as well as in Manhattan.

The Big Idea is a process that works to mobilize all people for the mission of Jesus. It achieves the genius of the And by helping you create a curriculum that is both targeted to your context and reproducible for your next new site or church plant.

> The Big Idea is a process that works to create a curriculum that is both targeted to your context and reproducible for your next new site or church plant.

5. CREATIVITY: PLANNED *AND* SPONTANEOUS

Brian Moll, lead pastor at Forefront Church in Manhattan, has been using the Big Idea for one year. I like the way Brian puts it: "Most churches plan about three days out. By planning nine weeks out, you increase your time to prepare by, say, fifty-nine days! That is significant. I have less stress and get better content."

For church leaders, having that much lead time as a result of advance planning is enough to make them want to change old habits. But occasionally I'll hear, "What about spontaneity? What if you sense God wants something different than what you started planning two months ago? And what if some local or national crisis takes place? What then?" Good questions. The Big Idea is a paradox: it is both planned and spontaneous.

Planning Makes for Less Stress

Let's face it, the reason most churches don't plan further in advance is because the lead pastor doesn't make it happen. And that's the one person who could benefit the most! Before we implemented the Big Idea process, I could never go out on Saturday night because I would still be tweaking my message. Planning the Big Idea in advance and working with a team to get messages done in advance have greatly reduced the stress in my life. If you are on the teaching team at your church, for no other reason than reduced stress, you should apply the advance planning aspect of the Big Idea process.

If you are currently using a week-to-week planning model, your volunteers are also feeling the stress of "get it done by this weekend" planning. Hank Brooks, lead pastor at Coastal Community Church in Virginia Beach, has been using the Big Idea process for a couple of years. He remembers what it was like before the Big Idea:

> Planning the Big Idea in advance and working with a team to get messages done in advance have greatly reduced the stress in my life.

The stress of planning one week out was taking its toll on our volunteers. I remember one instance where we thought up a great video drama idea — perfect for the topic of the coming Sunday. Our video team leader put in over thirty hours that week filming and editing that clip so we could play it Sunday. Two weeks later, we thought up another great video idea — that one only took about eighteen hours to produce. But the constant and urgent demands took their toll and our video team leader resigned. We haven't had her back on the video team since — and it's been over two years now.

Planning Means Less Wasted Time

When you follow the Big Idea process and do advance planning, you waste less time. Why? You no longer spend that first day in the office asking, "Okay, what are we going to do next weekend?" You know what you're going to do next weekend. Not only do *you* know what you're doing; everyone knows! The lead pastor, the worship pastor, the children's pastor, the students' pastor, the small group leader, the greeter at the front door — everyone knows what the Big Idea will be next week. Since the Big Idea is already decided, you waste less time picking out the theme of the next celebration service and spend more time preparing for it.

Planning Allows for More Creativity

"Oh, you know what we should have done . . ." How many times have you heard these words after a worship service? And the idea would have been brilliant, but it was too late. Or how many times have you had your own brilliant idea, but since you're planning each week for the coming weekend, you don't have enough time to organize it, script it, order it, or create it? Again the problem is planning. By planning weeks in advance, you have plenty of time to develop the brilliant idea you have today for a future Big Idea.

For one weekend we decided that for us to create an image that would really impact people, we needed to do a musical theater production that involved a wedding ceremony. We had the bride in white and the groom in a tux, accompanied by the bridesmaids and groomsmen. The creative teams not only pulled off this spectacular moment, but they did it at multiple locations! We never could have accomplished this production if we had thought of it on Tuesday and tried to make it happen by the weekend. And even if we had tried to pull it off in such a short time frame, I'm afraid the quality would have been very poor.

Hank Brooks says that the advance planning made possible by the Big Idea not only reduces stress but also increases creativity. He explains:

We were regularly struck with creative ideas we just didn't have time to pull off. The Big Idea gives us more time to plan and react to changing circumstances. It allows us to think bigger and more innovatively. What you can do in nine weeks is a lot better than what you can do in one week. For example, we now have added a writing team to our drama ministry that works on writing original material for our services. When you're one week out, it's hard enough memorizing a script, let alone writing one and learning it.

Planning Allows for Spontaneity

When it comes to planning, the Holy Spirit can work weeks in advance just as well as in the moment. Advance planning is what creates space for spontaneity to occur. You already know how to get things done the same week, right? So if there is a local or national crisis and you need to make an adjustment, do it. When the September 11 attacks occurred, we postponed our planned Big Idea and dealt with the Big Idea that life brought us. The weekend following 9/11, we chose the simple question "Why?" as our Big Idea and planned a celebration service that we had to pull off in one week. On those occasions when you're sure that God is taking you in a different direction than you planned several weeks ago, do what God tells you to do. Remember, the Big Idea is a tool. Let me say that again — it is just a tool for you to use to transform people into Christ followers. The Big Idea is not the boss — you are!

> Remember, the Big Idea is a tool for you to use to transform people into Christ followers. The Big Idea is not the boss — you are!

If you were to visit us at Community Christian Church, you would find that we are always making adjustments to the original Big Idea in order to improve on it. Maybe you're thinking, "But aren't you planning everything in advance?" We are. One of the benefits of the Big Idea is that when it comes to creativity, it is both planned *and* spontaneous!

6. CHRIST FOLLOWERS: MORE *AND* MORE MATURING

It makes me crazy the way we use the word *Christian* to describe anyone who is saved and *disciple* or the phrase *being discipled* for more committed Christians. The distinction seems to lower the bar for entrance into Jesus' mission and endorse mediocrity. But I already covered that back in chapter 1. So at the risk of undoing everything I hope to have done so far, let me introduce a final paradox and benefit of the Big Idea. The Big Idea develops more Christ followers *and* more mature Christ followers.

More

Since we first started using the Big Idea process at Community Christian Church eight years ago, we've seen our church grow by more than 500 percent. We've also seen the birth and development of the NewThing Network. The journey to this point has been simply amazing! Most of the people we are reaching were previously unchurched and are now finding their way back to God. Why? One of the reasons is the Big Idea.

Karen Brown, who recently moved to Boston as a part of a NewThing Network church-planting team, was not a Christ follower and was far from God when she first showed up at Community Christian Church. She describes how the Big Idea first impacted her: "One week in the service, Dave challenged those who were ready to believe and weren't baptized to leave the service right then and sign up to be baptized. I had always thought that I wasn't 'good enough,' but I realized that morning that God calls us right where we are. My sister and I were baptized together." If you were to ask Karen, she would tell you that the Big Idea helped her find her way back to God. One of the benefits of the Big Idea is more Christ followers.

We are discovering that more people are coming to church because the Big Idea just has a buzz about it. People like it, and because they like it, they talk about it. Consequently, word-of-mouth invitations to Community Christian Church increase simply because people like the concept of one Big Idea that everyone experiences in an age-appropriate setting. It makes sense to people.

When we started CCC, we interviewed literally thousands of unchurched people in our community. One of the biggest desires of that group was that we provide religious education for their children. I know that sounds weird coming from a group of unchurched people, but that's what they said. (Maybe I shouldn't be surprised; they knew a church was asking them the question!) Most of them (70 percent) grew up going to church, and many told us stories that were not positive. Many of them gave church a second try once they had kids and had a less-than-positive experience. They were looking for a way to fulfill their responsibility of "getting their kids some religious education," but many of them ended up just shushing their kids the whole time. When people hear about the Big Idea, they're excited; it's meeting a real need, and as a result, it's creating a buzz.

The Big Idea also has an empowering quality that increases the evangelistic potential of every Christ follower. It empowers parents because they are applying the same Big Idea to their lives that their children are applying. Often parents learn about the Big Idea in a weekend service and then discuss and experience it in a small group; their increased knowledge of the topic then gives them confidence to enter into spiritual conversations with their children. Likewise, the Big Idea empowers students to initiate spiritual con-

> The Big Idea has an empowering quality that increases the evangelistic potential of every Christ follower.

versations with their parents. Many students and young adults who attend CCC have been followers of Jesus for some time, while their parents are just starting on their journeys.

Maturing

It's not just about "more"; it's about more Christ followers committed to the mission of Jesus. And when you see more and more people committed to the mission, it's a sign that they are maturing spiritually. The Big Idea is relentless in making sure that people are not just getting information but experiencing transformation. If learning is enhanced through repetition of experience, then the Big Idea should teach! In the course of one week, people might have each of the following experiences related to one Big Idea:

> The Big Idea is relentless in making sure that people are not just getting information but experiencing transformation.

- Attend a celebration service centered on the Big Idea
- Have their kids experience the same Big Idea in Kids' City
- Attend a small group where they discuss the Big Idea
- Work through a family resource with their family on the same Big Idea
- Download a Podcast of the Big Idea teaching
- Watch a webcast of a "short film" related to the Big Idea
- Receive a scheduled weekly prerecorded phone call from the lead pastor regarding the Big Idea

None of this is new information; it is remarkably repetitive. But the repetition serves to ensure that every person is very clear on what Jesus is calling us to do or to be. The Big Idea creates a buzz that attracts more people and issues a call that transforms us into followers of Jesus.

Remember Karen, who relocated to be part of a church-planting team in Boston? She explains the maturing impact of the Big Idea in her life:

> The thing that is so great about the Big Idea is its relevance to what is going on in my life and the world *right now*. There were many weeks after service when I couldn't believe that the one thing I needed to hear, or the one thing I was struggling with, was the very same thing the message was on. I'll never forget the week on being "Water Walkers." It just happened to be the same time we were praying about the move to Boston to plant a church. The Big Idea and the challenges put out were the reasons I began serving, got baptized, began tithing, and decided to join the team in Boston.

Karen is a great example of how the Big Idea produces more Christ followers *and* more mature Christ followers.

Andy Stanley, Reggie Joiner, and Lane Jones, in *Seven Practices of Effective Ministry*, describe the paradox of the Big Idea. They challenge churches to teach less to get more:

> When we say "teach less for more" we mean that you should rethink what and how you communicate to your team. If "narrow the focus" suggests that you make a stronger impact when you do less, "teach less for more" implies that you can drastically improve how much people learn if you teach less. That doesn't necessarily mean that you say fewer words, but rather that you narrow the scope of what you teach to cover less information. In some cases, you will actually say more about fewer things. But here's the key: The things you choose to teach should be limited to those things that your people need to hear, in other words, the core principles most appropriate to your target audience. These are what we refer to as the "irreducible minimums" of learning.[6]

That's the Big Idea!

CHAPTER 5

CHANGING CHURCHES
ONE BIG IDEA
AT A TIME

Perhaps you've had this experience at a conference, or while checking out a church during a scheduled visit, or even while reading a book like this one. You learn about some fantastic new idea — the thing that is going to solve all of your problems — and it looks so shiny and glossy that you wish you could peek under the hood when nobody was looking. "It just can't be this [easy, seamless, simple, etc.]!" I tend to be rather cynical when it comes to churches that spend a whole lot of time telling other churches how green their grass is, so it's with a fair amount of reservation that I write this book.

Because we've waited so long to write on the benefits of the Big Idea, we at Community Christian Church have had the opportunity to track the paths of other innovative churches doing all or parts of the Big Idea. The scenario looks like this: A cool church will hang out with us for a few days. We'll ask them what they're doing to reach people. Then we'll steal their ideas. Occasionally they'll ask us what we're doing, we'll tell them, and then they'll steal our ideas. This experience is a beautiful thing called networking.

The scope of the Big Idea can be daunting sometimes, and many of you reading may feel as though your church staff or leaders will suffer from "forest for the trees" syndrome if you pitch such a "big" idea at the next meeting. So not only will this chapter offer some "buyer beware" stories from other churches that have experimented with the Big Idea; it will also give you a glimpse into how adaptable the Big Idea is to your church's culture. We hope you will find it to be very adaptable.

OPEN SOURCE

The Big Idea as a concept is an open source program. It is available to all and designed to be shaped by the end user. Mark Batterson and his team at National Community Church in Washington, D.C., visited Community Christian Church and attended several Big Idea meetings before implementing their own version of the Big Idea in September 2003. Here's what Mark has to say about their decision to implement the Big Idea:

> We felt like it was a stewardship issue. We've got hundreds of people giving us sixty minutes of their time each weekend. We want to maximize impact. I have a personal conviction: the most important truths ought to be communicated in the most unforgettable ways. Big Idea helps us accomplish that. Sometimes more is less and less is more. Most churches try to say too much each week. We've tried to say more by saying less. That's what the Big Idea is all about. We want to be laser-focused each week.
>
> Big Idea meetings have helped us package our sermon series more effectively. And the greatest truths ought to come in the best packages!

The leaders of National Community Church plan in advance, but not necessarily nine weeks out. They plan based on the series and then coordinate efforts between teaching, arts, music, hospitality, and environment for each series as a whole. Planning series to series puts them a month or so in advance of each weekend. While on occasion they have created a small group curriculum that links to the Big Idea, in most cases, they do not have any other Big Idea links. The congregation is young, with few families with children, and while the children's ministry staff members are aware of the Big Idea, they don't link their curriculum to it.

> "And the greatest truths ought to come in the best packages!"

If you would like to become a Big Idea church, it is not an all-or-nothing decision. Just like National Community Church, you can begin to apply what works best for your church starting today. In becoming a Big Idea church, you can go through at least three stages.

BIG: *B* IS FOR *BASIC*

National Community Church did not try to adapt the Big Idea instantly in every facet of its current organization. Its step toward the Big Idea was simple — a basic move that involved the decision to link whatever happens in its weekend services to one major idea and to link the environments surrounding those services as well.

For those of us who can't see the forest for the trees when it comes to implementing change, the first step is to think Basic. What is the first, definitive way in which your environment can take what are currently several little ideas and craft them into one Big Idea? For National and many others, the Basic move has occurred within the hour or so each weekend that constitutes their adult large group celebration experience.

> For those of us who can't see the forest for the trees when it comes to implementing change, the first step is to think Basic.

This becomes the seed from which one tree is grown. Will it become a forest? Only God knows, but you have to start somewhere, and it might as well be there.

Certainly this was true of Christian Community Church. When we began planning nine weeks in advance, it was only within the framework of the adult celebration service. The additional branches on the tree came later, one after the other over time. In fact, we also on occasion have cut a branch or two in order to salvage the tree. We spent one season of ministry developing the elementary curriculum for our Kids' City ministry, knowing we would need to invest all of our resources there. To make it happen, we elected to pull from outside sources for our preschool curriculum. Yes, you heard right: even at CCC there have been times when we weren't all focused on the same Big Idea.

Looking at the whole forest and not at the trees could keep you from implementing the Big Idea. When the leaders at Coastal Community Church in Virginia Beach first began using the Big Idea process to plan their weekend services, their main goal was to switch from planning one week out to planning eight weeks out. Hank Brooks, the lead pastor at Coastal, describes the process:

> When we came across the Big Idea strategy at Community Christian Church, we were planning only one week in advance. It took nearly two months to get our planning eight weeks out. During that two-month work-up phase, we committed to planning relatively simple services so that we had time in our meetings to advance to an eight-week planning window. We sacrificed a short-term decrease in quality (not a major decrease) that now allows us to experience significantly better quality on a week-to-week basis.

The leaders at Coastal are now in the process of implementing their version of the Big Idea within their children's ministry. In addition, they are developing a support/recovery ministry that will follow the Big Idea as well. Coastal is moving from Basic to Integrated.

BIG: *I* IS FOR *INTEGRATED*

Without underestimating the significance of the first step of creating one Big Idea per service, the next step is finding processes that will allow for another branch on the tree to grow. We call this the Integrated stage because you will integrate the Big Idea into more than one branch of your ministry. This step often involves additional staffing and recruiting of teams, as well as a whole lot of vision casting. When Coastal Community Church started following the Big Idea process, it transitioned from having one or two people developing services to having a thirteen-person volunteer team meeting once a week to plan services that would take place eight weeks later. As the leaders at Coastal move to integrate the children's ministry with the Big Idea, they will be recruiting additional staff, and it's likely they will need to create new brainstorming teams as well.

> We call this the Integrated stage because you will integrate the Big Idea into more than one branch of your ministry.

When Community Christian Church integrated the children's and students' ministries with the Big Idea, we invited the children's and students' staff to the existing Big Idea meeting. Many of these staff members, while on the same team for some time, had never attended this particular meeting. The first several weeks became a training ground for us and for them as we "got used to each other." The brainstorming was a bit forced at first, but after a while, we were able to get into a great groove with the topics. We would strongly encourage any church moving to the Integrated stage to begin with simultaneous meetings, for a couple of reasons.

First, a different kind of synergy emerges when teammates who play different positions are in the same room, working on the same project. The best ideas come from the unlikeliest of sources. Many times at CCC, the best Kids' City ideas have come from someone in Student Community, and vice versa. Many times in the early phases, we would intentionally mix up the teams to get the creative juices flowing even more.

Second, you have a better chance of streamlining ideas when those ideas are created at the same time. There have been many times in CCC's Big Idea history when the same video feature has been used in two or more of our venues and with different age groups. This is one of the great benefits of reaching the Integrated stage. The video that worked for the adults may work for Student Community or even Kids' City — but you'll never know if you plan in a vacuum. So plan together, and take advantage of the opportunity to share resources.

When we planned the family series mentioned in chapter 4, we chose to focus one week on Kids' City and the next on Student Community. We brought all the teams together for planning and created products that all of us would be able to use together. This kind of collaboration is what the Big Idea is all about, and it translates into products that your church will be confident bringing to the unchurched — products not possible without that level of integration.

> The video that worked for the adults may work for Student Community or even Kids' City — but you'll never know if you plan in a vacuum.

After a couple of years of growth, CCC was ready to have the adults', students', and children's Big Idea meetings take place at different times so that more individual time could be devoted to each age group. However, we asked at least one person to attend all three meetings, acting as a sort of conduit to allow for the sharing of ideas and resources. Churches in the Integrated phase must have open communication among all parties contributing to the Big Idea.

Early on in our Integrated phase, we missed the boat on open communication big-time. Our mistake was leaving out the Kids' City and Student Community leaders from some of our early planning. The final phase of brainstorming was reserved for the teaching team and lead pastors only. At the time, we didn't see the ramifications of not having a Kids' City or Student Community representative present. But what resulted was less ownership of the Big Idea in those two groups, creating a bit of an "us and them" culture. We paid the price. Two years ago we corrected that mistake, and the outcome has been exceptional. All teams are experiencing much more ownership, much less of an "us and them" feel, and considerably more collaboration. We can't believe we didn't think of it sooner.

BIG: G IS FOR GLOBAL

Are you ready to go global? When your church is buzzing with the Big Idea, rocking with topics that work for the whole church, and humming with age groups that receive the Big Idea in their language, you'll soon be ready to take that Big Idea and go global. You should consider creating a network that is able to do together that which you and others cannot do alone.

More and more churches are coming to realize that the best way to reach people far from God is to become a reproducing church that plants new churches. Community Christian Church believes strongly in the importance of reproducing and has a church-planting strategy in place through our NewThing Network. Many well-intentioned churches have a strategy that includes staffing, funding, and praying for the successful launch of their church plants. But after the launch, the strategy becomes one big "Good luck out there, cowboy!" from the launching church.

> You should consider creating a network that is able to do together that which you and others cannot do alone.

It doesn't have to be that way! If the church plant has a similar culture, why not collaborate with its leaders to develop each week's Big Idea? A young church can benefit from such a relationship with an established congregation, and the established church will benefit from the "on fire" vibe of the church planters. At CCC, the NewThing Network was formed to do exactly that: be a catalyst for a movement of reproducing churches. Through the network we have now launched five new churches, in Denver, Bakersfield (California), Detroit, Manhattan, and Boston. All of these churches work together with CCC to craft each week's Big Idea, and as Brian Moll of Forefront Church in Manhattan can attest, the collaboration makes

> If the church plant has a similar culture, why not collaborate with its leaders to develop each week's Big Idea?

a lot of sense for a church planter: "I believe that doing things like planning messages and series and creative elements should happen in community. Maybe one or two of us could have one grand idea by ourselves that we could implement once or twice a year, but when we all get together and brainstorm, think, pull at each other, and challenge one another, we grow spiritually, mentally, intellectually, and emotionally."

But the Big Idea not only creates collaboration; it also creates space for a church planter to "do what needs to be done" in the early phases of a church's life. Brian says:

> When done in community and through collaboration, [planning the Big Idea in advance] gives you more time to do other things, such as recruit and develop new leaders and artists. Our goal is to be a church that reproduces artists and leaders, congregations, campuses, and churches all over NYC. When we're not wrapped up with 80 percent of our time going to planning a one-hour service, we are freed up for conversations with leaders, apprentices, potential leaders, and, hello, people who don't know Christ yet, too!

Dave Richa of Jacob's Well Community Church in suburban Denver also speaks of collaboration and the way in which his church plant has benefited from the Big Idea: "As a lead pastor, I have a lot of things competing for my time and energy. To have confidence in a process that will put together an excellent message and a compelling program takes a lot off of my mind on a weekly basis. I also believe being in close proximity with other gifted leaders has matured me as a leader and has helped mature me as a follower of Christ."

So how do you go global? Well, I would love to tell you about the fancy integrated national and international internet systems that CCC employs in order to make

> The bottom line is, when there is commitment, communication, and collaboration among teams, even teams from churches across the country can work together to develop the same Big Idea.

collaboration happen across the United States. But right now, the process is quite simple and very low tech. A conference call, some instant-message chat rooms, and a bunch of document drafts emailed back and forth each week — that's what we do to go global. The bottom line is, when there is commitment, communication, and collaboration among teams, even teams from churches across the country can work together to develop the same Big Idea.

PART THREE

• • • •

Create Your Own Big Idea

CHAPTER 6

CREATING YOUR ONE-YEAR BIG IDEA PLAN

"Wow, you guys must be really organized!" is the comment I often hear when I tell people that we plan our Big Idea one year in advance. I wish that were the case. The creative chaos and last-minute scrambling that take place every week, as well as our love of anything new, tell the truth about us — we are not by nature a very organized group of leaders and artists. Before we started our one-year Big Idea plan, we had brainstorming meetings at which the worship team would come up with ideas that were unrelated to the ideas of the teaching team. We had musicians and actors who were not getting their music or scripts ahead of time. We had all kinds of ideas that couldn't be implemented on time. And in the middle of this disorganization, Christian Community Church was in the planning stages of adding a second site!

So how do we do it? We may not have an inclination for organization, but we have developed a "culture of discipline." In *Good to Great*, Jim Collins describes it this way: "When you put these two complementary forces together — a culture of discipline with an ethic of entrepreneurship — you get a magical alchemy of superior performance and sustained results."[1]

When it comes to the Big Idea, we at CCC stick to the plan. Whatever we lack in organization, we make up in sheer determination. We

> Whatever we lack in organization, we make up in sheer determination. We are not afraid to say, "Whatever it takes."

are not afraid to say, "Whatever it takes." We know the benefits of the Big Idea process, so we do everything in our power to make it happen week after week. You don't have to be organized to see the Big Idea become a reality; you just have to be determined to set finish lines and cross them.

So are you ready to plan your own Big Idea? Where do you start? At CCC, our ministry season starts in September and wraps up in August, so we begin by thinking about the entire year.

TWELVE MONTHS OUT: BIG IDEA BRAINSTORMING AND DECISION MAKING

Your mission, should you choose to accept it, is to plan your topics one year in advance. At first, this task might seem daunting, perhaps even impossible. But here's how to start.

The Creative Brainstorming Gathering

If you've decided that the Big Idea is for you, then you know the benefits. And if you have moved beyond the Basic stage and toward the Integrated stage, you have decided to have your adults, students, and children all following the same Big Idea. So let's see what it would take to start with the Integrated stage. The first step is to bring together representatives from each group that will implement the Big Idea (the adults', students', and children's ministries and perhaps other ministries such as support/recovery, seniors, etc.). At CCC, we invite these representatives (staff or volunteers) to a brainstorming gathering so that we can get their creative input for potential Big Ideas in the upcoming year. The goal of this gathering is threefold:

1. to brainstorm potential Big Ideas — the more minds the better;
2. to give each area that will implement the Big Idea ownership in the process; and
3. to package all of these Big Ideas into series of generally three to six weeks.

In that initial brainstorming gathering, we encourage any and every idea: ideas that people have thought up on their own and ideas that other churches have implemented. We write every one of these ideas on giant sticky notes as a way to validate them, and we save them for the next meet-

> At CCC, we extend an open invitation to any staff member in any ministry to attend these brainstorming gatherings.

ing. At CCC, we extend an open invitation to any staff member in any ministry to attend these brainstorming gatherings. They are big; we go through a lot of oversize sticky notes! Brainstorms might include fully developed themes and titles, such as the following:

God's Reality Shows

- *Fear Factor* vs. *Faith Factor*
- *The Apprentice* vs. *The Servant*
- *The Amazing Race* vs. ?
- *Survivor* vs. ?
- *Bachelor/Bachelorette* vs. ?

Or they might be much less developed — topics that we might want to explore over several weeks, but without any particularly catchy titles, such as the following:

The Holy Spirit

- Who is he?
- What does he do?

- When does he show up?
- Where is he?
- Why does he exist?
- How does he work?

These brainstorms should be very loose — allow the discussion to go anywhere, and try to keep the ideas from developing too much form. The wider the net, the more options you'll have when it comes to making the final decisions on the year's topics.

The Decision-Making Meeting

After the initial brainstorming gathering, a few key decision makers should take all of this great creative energy and determine the Big Ideas for the upcoming year. This group should include the lead pastor, any key teaching pastors who have theological influence in your church, and any people who have the best interests of children and students in mind. We encourage you to keep this group of decision makers very small. They will need to make tough decisions on themes and timing and will need to cast a vision for the teams that support their decisions. Since every church in our NewThing Network uses the same Big Ideas, the lead pastors from each of these churches are invited annually to join this group of decision makers.

Three tools are absolutely essential for this decision-making meeting: (1) a large calendar for the entire year, (2) a list of the potential Big Ideas in series format from the creative brainstorming gathering, and (3) lots of prayer.

Step 1: Prayer

We always open the meeting with prayer. If there is one time of the year when you really want to hear from God, it's now. You are about to determine the teaching ministry of your church for an entire year. What you decide to include and exclude will impact hundreds or even thousands of lives and will make a difference for all of eternity. In recent years we have scheduled this decision-making meeting at the end of a retreat during which the lead pastors have gone away for prayer, peer mentoring, and reflection on the ways that God wants us to lead our churches into the future.

Step 2: Consider the Calendar

After opening with prayer, we begin the meeting by making our own calendar

> If there is one time of the year when you really want to hear from God, it's now. You are about to determine the teaching ministry of your church for an entire year.

on giant sticky notes and posting it on the wall for all to see. Then we note any key dates on the calendar with the following considerations in mind: What are the optimal times for inviting newcomers? What day of the week is Christmas this year? What Sunday is Easter? Are there other days we want to acknowledge, such as Mother's Day? Are there other denominational or seasonal occasions we need to consider? We mark the calendar with those key dates because they will more than likely shape the "when" for some of our Big Ideas.

Step 3: Review and Rank the Possibilities

Then we use the third essential tool, a list of all of our potential Big Idea series from our creative brainstorming gathering. Since most of what we do is topical and not expository teaching, we will discuss the merit and value of each potential Big Idea series and then rank them. Now, there are times when it is clear that the Big Idea won't work for every age group or every location. These are by far the exception. In these cases, sometimes we discard the idea for the priority of creative collaboration, and sometimes we agree to go separate ways for a couple of crucial topics for each age group. I'm often asked, "How do you decide which Big Idea topics to use and which not to use?" "Where does the buck stop?" "Who has the final say?" We don't really think or behave like that. Every person in the decision-making meeting has an opportunity to voice his or her opinion. Some years we have used a numbering system to allow everyone to rank the top five topics. Other years we have polled the group by asking them to vote for the Big Idea topics we *must* do. But the final prioritizing of Big Idea topics every year comes through the consensus of a team built on solid relationships and genuine trust.

> The final prioritizing of Big Idea topics every year comes through the consensus of a team built on solid relationships and genuine trust.

Step 4: Place the Big Ideas on the Calendar

Even after you have a consensus on which Big Idea series are top priority, you still have work to do. Now you have to try to fit those series into the calendar for the next year. This is when you address questions such as the following: "How many weeks in a row should we hit on stewardship?" "When is the best time to do this series on relationships?" "Is Easter a 'stand-alone' week, or should it be the beginning of a series to encourage newcomers to return?" "How should we plan the summer, when people are more likely to miss one or more weeks of a Big Idea series?" As these and other questions are answered, we plot our Big Idea themes and topics on the calendar for the upcoming year.

At CCC, most of our topics cover an average of four weeks. On average, your team will be planning only ten to fourteen series per year. When you take note of Christmas and Easter and surround these dates with the themes that reflect your culture and your mission as a church, you'll be amazed at how fast the selection process can go and how many ideas you'll leave on the cutting room floor. But save them! You'll want them for next year's brainstorming gathering.

Here is a one-year Big Idea plan we used at CCC:

ONE-YEAR BIG IDEA SERIES: FEBRUARY 2004–JANUARY 2005

FEBRUARY

7–8	The Truth about God, Part 1 "I Refuse to Be Reduced"
14–15	The Truth about God, Part 1 "I'm Not to Be Taken Lightly"
21–22	The Truth about God, Part 1 "I Can Be Trusted and Enjoyed"
28–29	The Truth about God, Part 1 "I Care about Your Parents"

MARCH

6–7	The Story behind *The Passion of the Christ* The Hero: Who Was Jesus?
13–14	The Story behind *The Passion of the Christ* The Cast: What's Their Motivation?
20–21	The Story behind *The Passion of the Christ* The Plot: Why Did Jesus Die?
27–28	The Story behind *The Passion of the Christ* The Twist: What Difference Does the Resurrection Make?

APRIL

3–4	The Story behind *The Passion of the Christ* The Sequel: Where Is Jesus Now?
10–11	Relational Intelligence Experiencing Forgiveness (Easter)
17–18	Relational Intelligence Extending Acceptance
24–25	Relational Intelligence Practicing Encouragement

MAY

1–2	Relational Intelligence Managing Conflict
8–9	Relational Intelligence Envisioning Greatness
15–16	The Truth about God, Part 2 "All I Give Is Still Mine" (shall not steal)
22–23	The Truth about God, Part 2 "Marriage Is Sacred to Me" (shall not commit adultery)
29–30	The Truth about God, Part 2 "All Life Belongs to Me" (shall not murder)

JUNE

5–6	The Truth about God, Part 2
	"I Want You to Be What I Am" (shall not lie)
12–13	The Truth about God, Part 2
	"I'm Your Satisfaction" (shall not covet)
19–20	You Asked for It, Part 1: Q&A from the NewThing Network
	"How Can I Tell If Thoughts Are God's or My Own?"
26–27	You Asked for It, Part 2: Q&A from the NewThing Network
	"How Do I Know What I Was Born to Do?"

JULY

3–4	You Asked for It, Part 3: Q&A from the NewThing Network
	"What Would You Say to Someone with Depression or Mental Illness?"
10–11	You Asked for It, Part 4: Q&A from the NewThing Network
	"Why Do You Allow People to Suffer?"
17–18	Summer at the Lake (Conversations with Jesus)
	Follow the Leader
24–25	Summer at the Lake
	Weather the Storms

AUGUST

July 31–Aug. 1	Summer at the Lake
	Enjoy the Water
7–8	Summer at the Lake
	A Picnic for Five Thousand
14–15	Summer at the Lake
	Don't Miss the Boat
21–22	Headline News, Part 1 (topic TBD that week)
28–29	Headline News, Part 2 (topic TBD that week)

SEPTEMBER

4–5	Headline News, Part 3 (topic TBD that week)
11–12	Eternal Velocity
	Missional Velocity
18–19	Eternal Velocity
	Spiritual Velocity
25–26	Eternal Velocity
	Relational Velocity

OCTOBER

2–3	Eternal Velocity
	Courageous Velocity
9–10	Eternal Velocity
	Lifetime Velocity
16–17	Liking the One You Love
	Liking Your Mate/Date
23–24	Liking the One You Love
	Liking Your Kids
30–31	Liking the One You Love
	Liking Your Family

NOVEMBER

6–7	Liking the One You Love
	Liking Yourself
13–14	How to Ruin Your Finances in Two Words or Less
	The First Word: *More*
20–21	How to Ruin Your Finances in Two Words or Less
	The Second Word: *Mine*
27–28	The Power of a Moment
	Living in the Moment

DECEMBER

4–5	The Power of a Moment
	A Holy Moment
11–12	The Power of a Moment
	A Moment of Doubt
18–19	The Power of a Moment
	A Moment of Risk
25–26	The Power of a Moment
	From This Moment On

JANUARY

1–2	New Year's Revolutions
	The Ancient Revolutionary
8–9	New Year's Revolutions
	The Consuming Revolutionary
15–16	New Year's Revolutions
	The Relational Revolutionary
22–23	New Year's Revolutions
	The Unstoppable Revolutionary
29–30	New Year's Revolutions
	The Revolutionary Within

THIRTEEN WEEKS OUT: BIG IDEA GRAPHS

After the one-year Big Idea plan has been charted, we turn to the teaching/preaching arm of the church for development. Select those best suited for the role, and cast them as the writers of short essays that flesh out each series and each topic within that series. We call these essays Big Idea graphs. For many churches, the lead pastor is the primary teacher/preacher and will be the one responsible for creating such essays. At CCC, this role is delegated to our teaching team leader rather than the lead pastor. Although this role can be delegated, be sure that the apple doesn't fall too far from the tree. The content and theology of the Big Idea graphs are very important, because they will shape your church's culture and mission.

> The content and theology of the Big Idea graphs are very important, because they will shape your church's culture and mission.

For CCC, the graphs include an overall summary of each Big Idea series (no more than one page for each weekly topic), as well as the biblical foundation for the Big Idea, other important sources, and the basic response we want people to have. The graphs give the reader an opportunity to get at the heart of the series and the specific ideas behind it. Sure, a stewardship series is about money, but in what way? What angle will we take on the issue of tithing? What's the hook? How will we cleverly design the title to draw the unchurched? The graphs also include suggested "translations" of the topic to reach the hearts and minds of different age groups. Your children's ministry leaders should see a paragraph devoted to the Big Idea that kids should take away from the series, and your students' ministry leaders should see a paragraph devoted to teens.

Maybe the best way to describe a Big Idea graph is to let you see one:

BIG IDEA GRAPH: SEPTEMBER 2005

New Series: "Eternal Velocity: Living at the Speed of God"

Series Big Idea: So many people feel as though they're "going nowhere fast": their lives are filled with lots of effort and stress and strain and franticness, but they're just spinning their wheels. Eternal velocity is living life pursuing and experiencing the dream of God, where purpose, direction, and pace come from living a life in which a relationship with God is at the center of everything, including our lives as individuals and our relationships with others. Eternal velocity is moving through life on the trajectory and at the speed that God sets for our lives, which are eternity focused and driven.

Kids' City Series Idea: For kids, you might call this series "What in the World Am I Here For?" or "What Are We Doing Here?" In this series we will help kids learn that there is an alternative to living life just to be happy. Only God has the answer to the question, "What am I here for?": to love him and be close to him and to help others do the same.

September 11 – 12: "Missional Velocity"

Big Idea: Eternal velocity starts with understanding life as being driven by God's mission: to live not in search of self-fulfillment but in a continual, dynamic, personal relationship with God and to help others do the same.

In his book *It's Not about Me: Rescue from the Life We Thought Would Make Us Happy*, Max Lucado writes that missional velocity is what replaces our own checklists and wish lists that we think will bring us happiness but won't. Our own lists of wishes and wants only leave us either frantically "chasing after the wind" or disappointed and lethargic, wondering, "Is this all there is?"

This service will follow up our 3C leadership vision night, where Dave will lay out the direction and goals for CCC for the coming year (these goals are being formulated at the time this graph is being written). The main thrust will be that pursuing and extending God's kingdom both individually and together give our lives the purpose and direction and pace we could never have if we were living life only to find our own happiness and fulfillment in whatever ways we could. Any mission we have for ourselves apart from God's mission for us will never give us eternal velocity: any other mission will lead only to temporary fulfillment and ultimate dissatisfaction.

Scripture: "But you will receive power when the Holy Spirit comes on you; and you will be my witnesses in Jerusalem, and in all Judea and Samaria, and to the ends of the earth" (Acts 1:8).

"Be very careful, then, how you live — not as unwise but as wise, making the most of every opportunity, because the days are evil" (Eph. 5:15 – 16).

"The thief comes only to steal and kill and destroy; I have come that they may have life, and have it to the full" (John 10:10).

Here's what the Big Idea graphs are not: they are not programming ideas, song suggestions, or small group curriculum ideas. They need to stay brief, clear, and on topic — scholarly, developing the topic through the use of the Bible and other texts that support the idea. Try as best as you can to create a document that feels as universal as possible, while staying as close as you can to the Big Idea. Programming for those topics comes later.

Now that you've learned how to develop your Big Idea graphs, it's time to lift them from the page and shape them into weekend services, one week at a time.

CHAPTER 7

IMPLEMENTING YOUR BIG IDEA PLAN

Your Big Idea plan for the year is now in place, and you have begun the process of composing Big Idea graphs that highlight key points for each week. Now for the first time, you will be sending out these Big Ideas to your teams for perusal, in the hope that they will be able to take them and create new experiences based on their areas of expertise. This process can be somewhat unnerving; many people will be reviewing your writing, agreeing with it, disagreeing with it, and giving out not only opinions but also critiques. Theology disputes may even break out at this point. That's okay. A good Big Idea will always spark interest and discussion, resulting in kudos as well as criticism. That's the risk we take in sharing these Big Ideas with the world.

> A good Big Idea will always spark interest and discussion, resulting in kudos as well as criticism. That's the risk we take in sharing these Big Ideas with the world.

TEN TO THIRTEEN WEEKS OUT: DISTRIBUTION OF THE BIG IDEA GRAPHS

Here's how to start: Distribute the Big Idea graphs to all ministries that are responsible for the creative content of any large or small group. Give graphs to members of the music ministry so they can brainstorm ideas for worship songs and music specials for all ages. Do the same for script writers; allow them to brainstorm potential sketch or video ideas. Also distribute the graphs to the small group curriculum teams so they can begin the process of building small group tools that align with the graphs. At CCC, we have Big Idea small group discussion guides for adults, as well as small group curriculums for students and children that are designed around the Big Idea. We can begin this brainstorming ten to thirteen weeks out with complete confidence that we are all in agreement and directional alignment.

If each team can brainstorm one series at a time, meetings along those lines can take place every month or so, reducing the amount of time spent at later meetings that by nature will need to take place once a week. We've found that it's much easier, for example, to give the music team license to brainstorm song selections for a month at a time and then bring those ideas to the weekly Big Idea creative team meeting. Brainstorming in advance gives everyone a head start and prevents the weekly meeting from dragging on too long.

> **"Lead time is the key to creativity."**

The weeks between the time that the Big Idea graphs are distributed and the time that a specific service takes place are critical brainstorming weeks. Mark Batterson, lead pastor at National Church in Washington, D.C., explains:

> I think the beauty of the Big Idea is lead time. The lead time allows us to put together video trailers for our series. Meeting in a movie theater, we try to play off the "coming soon" and "trailer" ideas as part of our motif of being a church that meets in a movie theater. The Big Idea helps us come up with creative video ideas that often require several weeks to script, shoot, edit, and produce. The Big Idea also helps me read strategically. We decide on themes, and then I'll buy a dozen related books to help me prepare for the teaching component. Lead time is the key to creativity.

Use this lead time and take full advantage of the creative power your ministries can deliver every week.

NINE WEEKS OUT: BIG IDEA CREATIVE TEAM MEETING

Finally, we've arrived at the meeting for which you have been preparing — the Big Idea creative team meeting. This meeting is so important to the Big Idea process that we have devoted all of chapter 9 to it. But to continue the summary of the one-year Big Idea plan, let me give you a quick overview of this collaborative experience.

At CCC, we begin our Big Idea creative meeting by revisiting the topic using the graphs that were crafted four weeks ago. Then we creatively brainstorm every possible way for people to experience this Big Idea. I know it sounds cliché, but there are no bad ideas — not yet! Take these ideas and all of the ideas that your arts teams have brought with them and create experiences based on how your church "does church." Dream big: since the service is nine weeks away, you should have plenty of time to execute the ideas.

At CCC, we walk out of the Big Idea creative team meeting with a clear plan for the upcoming celebration service, including sketch/story development, special music, worship songs, video ideas, and the order of service, all the way down to how many minutes each segment should be. If we had to, we could take the heart of that meeting and execute the service that week. In other words, the plan is very specific. It may seem strange planning your Christmas series in October, but by planning so far in advance, you give yourself a huge advantage in implementing those ideas that could never be pulled off in one week.

Kerry Cox, the creative arts director at Jacob's Well Community Church, has been using the Big Idea for the last three years. He notes, "The nine weeks out has also improved scheduling of talent.... It helps to know if we have specific needs (characters for a drama that only certain actors can do, or a difficult guitar song that one guitarist would excel at) and whether those people are available. If they aren't, we have time to make other plans."

We currently have three Big Idea creative meetings — one for the adults' ministry, one for Student Community, and one for Kids' City so that each ministry can plan its large group celebration service. At CCC, all of these meetings happen once a week, on Tuesday, for about two hours each. All of these meetings have to be weekly so that the planning is always "nine weeks out." These meetings begin the cycle of knowing what is coming nine weeks in advance and having nine plates of services spinning in the air at the same time.

This pattern is flexible enough that it is easily embraced by all styles of worship. I've seen the Big Idea process work in the creation of traditional worship services, contemporary services, and services with and without drama, video, or dance. All styles can benefit from the Big Idea; in fact, a church that currently offers more than one adult style can greatly benefit by streamlining its styles into one Big Idea.

> All styles can benefit from the Big Idea; in fact, a church that currently offers more than one adult style can greatly benefit by streamlining its styles into one Big Idea.

FIVE WEEKS OUT: BIG IDEA REALITY CHECK

For the arts teams at CCC, the five-week point is the first big reminder of what we planned a month ago. It serves as a reality check after we've planned an amazing Big Idea experience. This is when we ask questions such as the following: "Is that video clip available yet?" "Can we create that prop?" "Can we really afford live camels?" And since we schedule our artists by the month, we are also able to ask ourselves, "Do we have the artists we need to pull off the Big Idea experience we created five weeks ago?" Most of the time we are able to implement what we have planned, but sometimes we look at what we planned and say, "Oh no!" and then make adjustments. Fortunately, when that happens, we still have five weeks to make any additional changes.

THREE WEEKS OUT: BIG IDEA TEACHING TEAM MEETING AND BIG IDEA DISCUSSION GUIDE

Big Idea Teaching Team Meeting

Like the Big Idea creative meeting, the Big Idea teaching team meeting is very important to the Big Idea process; in fact, we have devoted all of chapter 10 to it. But to avoid disrupting the flow of our summary of the one-year Big Idea plan, let me give you a brief description of the teaching team meeting. It brings together all individuals who are responsible for teaching and preaching. Lasting one hour and forty-five minutes (what I call the fastest 105 minutes of the week), the meeting involves brainstorming ideas for the message, structuring the message, and delegating the writing of each section to different members of the teaching team. Once team members have received their writing assignments, they each have one week to write their section of the message.

For the teaching team, this collaborative writing process is a very rewarding part of the one-year Big Idea plan. Many months ago some people on the team were part of the decision-making meeting that prioritized the Big Ideas for the upcoming year, and now they're coming together to craft a message that will fit perfectly within the celebration service designed around the Big Idea they selected.

Big Idea Discussion Guide

In the same way that our teaching team collaborates to create a teaching manuscript, the small group curriculum writers collaborate to create a discussion guide. Recently I was talking with a new believer in my small group, in which we use the Big Idea discussion guide, and he told me, "It really helps to hear other people's thoughts about the same Big Idea." These discussion guides, which are used by individuals, families, and small groups, reinforce the Big Idea that people experienced the weekend before.

TWO WEEKS OUT: BIG IDEA TEACHING MANUSCRIPT AND BIG IDEA MEDIA

Big Idea Teaching Manuscript

With two weeks left to go, the teaching team has completed its first edition of the teaching manuscript; we call it the "1.0." With the Big Idea process, there are no more late Saturday nights searching the internet for sermon ideas; no more begging God to please give us something important to say. Dave Richa, lead pastor at Jacob's Well Community Church, puts it this way: "In my three years as lead pastor at JWCC, I have never had to say, 'Oh no, what am I going to say tomorrow at church? Let me see what Hybels or Warren said last week.' I am consistently surrounded by a group of synergistic people who are driven by the practical needs of the upcoming Big Idea."

If you have ever done any teaching or preaching on a regular basis, imagine being prepared with a manuscript two weeks before you have to deliver it. It's a beautiful thing! Part of the beauty is that you have two more weeks to add or subtract from the manuscript, insert illustrations and personal anecdotes, and tweak the flow to make it match your personal style.

> "I am consistently surrounded by a group of synergistic people who are driven by the practical needs of the upcoming Big Idea."

Big Idea Media

All members of the teaching team have access to the 1.0 edition of the teaching manuscript so that they can ask the media team to create PowerPoint slides with graphics, Scripture references, and any other visual reinforcement of the teaching. These requests are emailed to volunteers who do the initial work of searching the internet for visual content and who then forward their findings to the media team for final editing.

Two weeks before a specific service, the media team crosses the finish line for the production of any videos for children, students, or adults. With so much advance preparation, no teaching pastor or children's leader will ever see the video for the first time on Sunday morning. Having the videos finished two weeks in advance allows us to maximize collaboration and integration between the media team and the teaching team.

ONE WEEK OUT: THE BIG IDEA EXPERIENCE

One more "production" meeting is in order so that all teams will be on the same page with the content for the large group experiences for all ministries. Again, for CCC, these meetings take place on Tuesdays. Once the plans are confirmed, staff and volunteers contact artists to make sure they are ready, the media and teaching teams make last-minute edits to videos and manuscripts, and the arts teams conduct rehearsals in the various art forms.

At CCC, the NewThing Network churches also collaborate during this week. Many times, one of the churches will complete a video project and then upload it to the web and make it available for download. Collaboration and sharing are high values for us, because they allow us to achieve the best product possible. Recently a NewThing church discovered a new video clip to use as a segue from the teaching time that far surpassed the clip proposed in our original nine-weeks-out plan. The Big Idea is not rigid: we have the opportunity to download a new clip, check it out, and then decide whether to replace our original idea. That's exactly what we did, and all of the NewThing churches benefited from one church's initiative. And since all of us were focused on the same Big Idea, we were able to collaborate very efficiently in that moment.

Do we always cross our finish lines? Of course not — we aren't *that* organized (or disciplined). But when push comes to shove, the Big Idea happens in the allotted time frame at least 85 percent of the time, and we can live with that. We still have opportunities for improvement, but our brainstorming meetings are on topic and not a waste of time. Our musicians and actors get their music and scripts far enough in advance to be prepared. And we have enough time to implement almost any idea we can think up. Creative collaboration has allowed us to maximize our missional impact, and it can do the same for your church.

> Collaboration and sharing are high values for us, because they allow us to achieve the best product possible.

CHAPTER 8

THE TWO MOST IMPORTANT PLAYERS IN THE BIG IDEA

Authors' note: Since Eric Bramlett and Dave Ferguson play the two roles described in this chapter, we asked Jon Ferguson to take the lead on this chapter and write it from his perspective.

Eric, the new creative arts director, had not been on staff for long, coming to Community Christian Church from the arts community in Chicago, in which he had directed a variety of shows for a number of theater companies. He came up with the idea of producing a play to encourage developing actors and also give those at CCC an opportunity to reach out to their friends.

The play Eric chose was titled *The Dining Room*, written by A. R. Gurney, a playwright who, as far as we know, is not a Christ follower. However, his play deals with topics very relevant to our audience — primarily the way that the family structure has deteriorated over time. The backdrop of the play is a dining room, and the audience is reminded that the dining room is the place where the American family would gather regularly, where everything seemed perfect (á la Walton's Mountain), and where family relationships were harmonious, at least for an hour. Contrast that idyllic picture with what Gurney's script says the dining room has become: a place where clothes are folded as they come out of the dryer, a place where people still might enjoy some food, but mainly by themselves as each person in the family rushes off to one activity after another.

Here's where the plot thickens. Eric tells the story like this:

> There was profanity in the script a couple of times with a couple of characters. Nothing major, but I certainly felt like in these situations, for these characters to be authentic, they needed to speak the words as written by the playwright. They simply wouldn't have said, "Doggone it," and needed to say something to express their feelings with authenticity. Actually, I changed some dialogue from a "more" offensive word to a slightly "less" offensive word. I felt like we needed to let the dialogue occur as written.

And Dave recalls the situation this way:

> When I walked into a rehearsal for the play, I was very impressed. The set was great, the story was strong, the actors were well prepared. Everyone seemed to love what was happening. I knew this was a dream come true for Eric to direct a live play that we could open up to the community. It was just a few minutes into the rehearsal when I heard some of the profanity. I got a lump in my throat. The last thing I wanted to do was be "Church Dad" and call the script into question. But my take on it was that this play had no real hard-core issues to deal with, so why pepper it with that kind of language? If we were staging *Schindler's List* and there was hard-core stuff to deal with, then it made sense — in that case it came with the territory — but not with this story.

TRUST AND RISK— TWO SIDES OF THE SAME COIN

Patrick Lencioni, in *The Five Dysfunctions of a Team*, says that the "absence of trust" makes it impossible to develop a great team. He writes:

> Unfortunately, the word *trust* is used — and misused — so often that it has lost some of its impact and begins to sound like motherhood and apple pie. That is why it is important to be very specific about what is meant by trust. In the context of building a team, trust is the confidence among team members that their peers' intentions are good and that there is no reason to be protective or careful around the group. In essence teammates must get comfortable with one another.[1]

Trust is much easier to talk about than to put into practice, especially for people in two roles that are often perceived as completely opposite. The archetype creative arts person is the "hardly ever on time, always trying to push the envelope, imaginative type with more ideas than could ever possibly be put into action." The archetype lead pastor is the "early to rise, quick to correct, stodgy, button-downed middle-aged athlete who just wants someone to be as passionate about church growth as him." These two people, the most important players in the Big Idea, have different names in different places, but they are most commonly called the lead pastor (or senior pastor) and the creative arts director (or worship pastor).

When it comes to the two key players in the Big Idea, two big words emerge as the flip sides of the same coin: *trust* and *risk*. Most people would agree that any thriving relationship requires tremendous amounts of trust and risk. This is particularly true of the relationship between the two most important players in the Big Idea process.

Artists need to take risks; the very nature of art is risky. When a musician plays a piece he composed, when a dancer performs a dance, when a painter displays her work, all risk the rejection or acceptance of the watching world. To do art is to be a risk taker. If artists are

> If artists are going to do art in the church, the leadership must trust the artists' judgment regarding which risks are worth taking and which risks are not.

going to do art in the church, the leadership must trust the artists' judgment regarding which risks are worth taking and which risks are not.

Leaders need trust. They are ever mindful of the big picture and the direction in which things are heading, and as they paint a compelling picture of an ideal future, they need followers to trust that they will always do what is in the best interest of the mission of the church. That trust will challenge all to take huge risks for the mission.

> No relationship in the church can be more volatile than the one between the lead pastor and the creative arts director. Consequently, these two key players must develop a high level of trust and willingness to take risks together.

No relationship in the church can be more volatile than the one between the lead pastor and the creative arts director. Consequently, these two key players must develop a high level of trust and willingness to take risks together. How are trust and risk taking fostered in the church? Following are descriptions of three factors that have contributed to Dave and Eric's great working relationship: planning, proximity, and parameters.

PLANNING

By now you should have a good grasp of our advance planning model. While your planning model may look dramatically different from ours, let me give you a quick recap of what advance planning looks like, because it will go a long way toward building a great relationship between the two key players in the Big Idea.

Advance planning provides an environment in which the relationship between the lead pastor and creative arts director can thrive. With themes developed nine to twelve months in advance and a nine-week window between ideas for a celebration service and the actual service, artists gain a sense of fulfillment, knowing that their job consists of more than simply cranking out a particular theme for the week. Advance planning gives artists time to perfect their crafts and to take the corresponding risks, while also allowing enough time for both the lead pastor and the creative arts director to trust the risk that they will take together. One of the great gifts a church can give its artists is the space or time to create.

Imagine if Michelangelo's supervisor came to him and said, "I love the mural idea, but you need to have that thing done by Sunday morning — it's Easter, and we're expecting our biggest crowds of the year." Maybe that sounds absurd, but with many of our current planning models, we expect our artists to create masterpieces yet give them only four or five days to do it. And when they do come up with creative (and risky) ideas in such a short time frame, often it's difficult for all parties to feel comfortable with the creative plan.

Here's my take on the advantages of our advance planning model and the way it impacts Dave and Eric's relationship. While our advance planning model may seem extremely disciplined and even rigid from an outsider's perspective, what we've discovered is that every creative person and lead pastor has a deadline of some kind. For many, it may be the Thursday before the Sunday service. We call it "game time," and let's be real, a lot of churches operate that way. Unfortunately, when

> Imagine if Michelangelo's supervisor came to him and said, "I love the mural idea, but you need to have that thing done by Sunday morning — it's Easter, and we're expecting our biggest crowds of the year."

your deadline is so close to "game day," you usually end up serving your deadline rather than the other way around. We have a weekly deadline just like every other church; however, we believe that because we set our deadlines weeks and even months in advance of "game time," our deadlines actually serve us. Not only that, but they give us tremendous relational freedom.

Advance Planning Gives Freedom to Think Creatively

The advance planning model gives all of us artists (that includes me, one of the teaching pastors) time to think creatively without feeling held back by the confining question, "How can we possibly pull that off by this weekend?" Week-to-week planning leads to higher levels of frustration on everyone's part, but with advance planning, artists can thrive, knowing they will have sufficient time to pull off even their greatest creative ideas. We like to think of each series and each celebra-tion service as a giant, blank palette waiting for the artist's paintbrush, and if the likelihood of our producing a masterpiece increases with more time to plan, then advance planning is well worth the effort.

Some might think that getting artists to be disciplined enough to plan so far in advance is next to impossible. What we've found is that once everyone agrees to a timetable and the artists begin to expe-rience the freedom within advance planning, they would never go back to working week to week. Advance planning actually sends the message, "We value you enough to give you the time you need to be creative! In addition, we'll put structures in place to cultivate your cre-ativity and hold you account-able to those structures." This is a huge relational deposit into the lives of our artists.

> Week-to-week planning leads to higher levels of frustration on everyone's part, but with advance planning, artists can thrive, knowing they will have sufficient time to pull off even their greatest creative ideas.

Advance Planning Gives Freedom to Suspend Skepticism

When planning takes place just days before "game day," skeptics can too easily say, "There's no way we can make that happen!" That's not necessarily a bad response. In fact, if you don't hear that from time to time, chances are you're not thinking big enough. Skepticism is our gut-level reaction when we can't imagine pulling off a great creative idea within the existing time constraints.

Advance planning minimizes the occurrence of this gut-level reaction. It also allows us to call a time-out, to suspend the skepticism for a few days or even weeks by saying, "That may be a great idea. Let's step back from it for a few days and do some legwork to see if it's possible for us to pull it off." With more time, we can think of and explore other creative possibilities. Often after we decide not to go with the original idea, a second or third more feasible option will emerge that is just as creative as the original idea and more doable. Advance planning allows us to suspend skepticism and take extra time to explore a new alternative.

One example of this benefit of advance planning at CCC had to do with the selection of a song. Eric is a big fan of the Bare-naked Ladies. If you don't know the group, don't throw down this book. They create some great music that I guarantee you would like — they just have a name that makes you roll your eyes. Eric wanted to do a song from their latest CD that was right on for an upcoming Big Idea. Dave had received some complaints the last time we featured one of their songs because the name "Barenaked Ladies" was printed in the program (we often reference the original artist). Dave didn't want more grief and reasoned that there had to be another song we could perform. Eric pushed back by asserting that the group's music is outstanding and that the people who had complained didn't even know of the group.

They were both right. The extra time in planning allowed them to suspend skepticism and consider a third option. If they would have had to make a win-lose decision right then in order to get the music out to the musicians on time, the result would have been a relational withdrawal. Either they wouldn't have taken the risk, or they would have experienced a breach of trust. The third option was this: often the Barenaked Ladies are called "BNL." So a few weeks later, the musicians performed the latest cut that was perfect for the Big Idea, and the name of the original artist printed in the program was "BNL." A win for everyone — a risk was taken and trust was intact.

Advance Planning Gives Freedom to Postpone Decisions

The previous example also illustrates another benefit of advance planning — freedom to wait before making an important decision. Using a week-to-week planning model tends to increase tension and decrease the opportunity for further collaboration and dialogue, particularly when it comes to tough decisions. There is a correlation between tension and creativity. While some people say they are at their creative best when they are up against a deadline, they are seldom at their relational best; they are likely highly stressed and not very fun to be around, resulting in increased tension. Tension

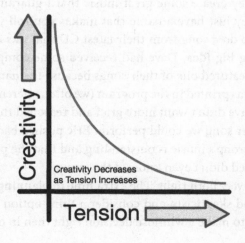

Creativity Decreases
as Tension Increases

stifles creativity and sets the table for much more relational conflict.

In a week-to-week planning model, often a great idea will surface that will require hours and hours to develop. As a result, someone is likely to say, "I need to know if we're going to do this or not, right now!" People in a pressure cooker environment have to make decisions quickly, because time is of the essence. An advance planning model affords people much more time to dialogue, pray, reflect, and seek wise counsel, thus minimizing the likelihood that someone will say, "I need to know right now!"

Having the opportunity to weigh the pros and cons of various options without having to make a call on the spot gives the creative arts director and lead pastor more opportunities to ask each other questions and engage in productive dialogue, and thus reduces the number of instances when someone (usually the lead pastor) has to make a call. The added benefit is that the two key players become comfortable making more decisions independently, because each has learned how the other person typically responds to particular ideas or situations.

> Having the opportunity to weigh the pros and cons of various options without having to make a call on the spot gives the creative arts director and lead pastor more opportunities to ask each other questions and engage in productive dialogue, and thus reduces the number of instances when someone (usually the lead pastor) has to make a call.

PROXIMITY

Community guru Randy Frazee, in *Making Room for Life* and *Connecting Church*, explains how proximity increases the depth of community in small groups. The idea is that the closer you actually live to the people in your small group, the greater the depth of community you will experience, because proximity increases the frequency of interaction.

Retailers understand this concept as well; the closer a store is to a customer, the more often that customer will frequent the store. They call the reverse concept "distance decay." For them, it means that the farther customers are from a particular store or outlet, the less loyalty they will have to that store. The concept of proximity helps stores like Target determine where to open a new store. Part of the equation is based on how far people will travel to a given store and remain loyal customers.

Willow Creek Community Church discovered something similar about its membership. Church leaders found that people who live beyond a thirty-mile radius from the South Barrington campus would, in spite of the distance, consistently celebrate on weekends, participate in a small group, and contribute financially. But those same people were not likely to invite a friend to celebrate with them, and they were less likely than those who lived closer to use their gifts to serve in a significant way. Their solution: launch sites that would leverage the advantages of proximity. As the twist on the old saying goes, "Distance makes the heart go yonder." (Or is it "wander"?) You get the point.

Let's take this idea to a micro level. Proximity is also important in a work environment, increasing the depth of community and loyalty to one another. When Eric, our creative arts director, first came on staff, Dave, the lead pastor, intentionally moved Eric's desk right next to his desk. He knew that Eric was going to play a pivotal role in the future of CCC, and he wanted to spend as much time with him as possible. Looking back, this move seemed small but was huge in the development of their relationship. When we moved into our first facility and needed to increase our focus on additional funding, Dave made sure his desk was next to that of Troy McMahon, who directed our finances at the time. He knew that fund-raising was going to be critical to CCC's accomplishment of what God had in mind for us in that next season, and he wanted to be as close to Troy as possible.

We have a unique office arrangement. No one has an individual office of his or her own, and most of our staff members share desk space with someone else. At our Naperville campus facility, affectionately known as the "Big Yellow Box" (because it's a cube-shaped building painted yellow), we have two rooms designated for office space. One room is about 500 square feet and includes space for twelve part-time and full-time

> When Eric, our creative arts director, first came on staff, Dave, the lead pastor, intentionally moved Eric's desk right next to his desk. He knew that Eric was going to play a pivotal role in the future of CCC, and he wanted to spend as much time with him as possible.

staff people. The other room is about 1,500 square feet, with space for twenty-five to thirty part-time and full-time staff people. Now, not all of these people are in the office at the same time (unless, of course, we're serving really great food for lunch). By the very nature of our office design, however, everyone is close to each other, and everyone

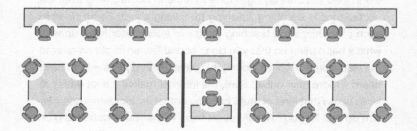

Diagram of Community Christian Church's Office Design. Most of our staff sit in quads, facing each other with no dividers.

is in each other's business. We often say that if you don't know what's going on, just sit at your desk for a few minutes and listen to the conversations around you. The downside is that if you're having a bad day, everybody knows about it — you can't hide!

With this arrangement, not only are Eric and Dave close to each other, but we're all close to each other. How does proximity impact Eric and Dave's relationship? Here's what Eric has to say:

> I think many churches have their arts teams and their pastoral teams so far apart that one doesn't know what the other is doing. As it relates to the Big Idea, this is dangerous, because it further implies that teaching is not an art and that pastors know nothing about art. Many times I've thought something out loud about an idea, or was working on a draft of a script, and in the moment, I wanted to be able to think out loud and get some feedback. Who better to get it from than the pastor? And if he's nearby, available, and accessible, that makes a huge statement about the value of that relationship. Don't get me wrong, I know sometimes people need a place to hide, and that's cool, but also find time to be around, in the mix, where the brainstorms are happening.
>
> One more thing about Dave and I being in close proximity to each other: Frankly, most teaching pastors don't stay in touch with pop culture. Maybe they don't have the time, or at least they don't think they have the time. Who really knows? Maybe they don't. If they have the time or not, let us do it for you. Any arts people worth their salt are staying in tune with the world, knowing what the unchurched is watching, listening to, talking about. Being close to each other helps the teaching pastor or lead pastor keep up with what's happening so that you don't sound like an idiot and refer to the lead singer of U2 as Boh-Noh. (Dave didn't do this — but I have heard it more than once.) Sure, the internet makes it a lot easier to keep up on that kind of stuff, but why not let your creative arts person do that for you? And if you let them know you're depending on them for that kind of information, chances are they will do a better job of staying on top of it themselves as well as recognizing another way you value their friendship and contribution to the team.

Dave explains three benefits of his and Eric's proximity to each other:

First, because of our proximity, we became friends more quickly. When I spent time with Eric and was interviewing him for the job of creative arts director, I knew we had found a special person. He helped start a theater company in Chicago, was an avid sports fan and a terrific power forward on the basketball court, and loves Jesus passionately. When hiring staff, my teammates have been coached to consider the three Cs of character, competency, and chemistry. For us, chemistry is always the first priority, but that chemistry must be fostered. Eric has become one of my best friends, and our being close to each other in proximity the first few months and years of his time on staff was a huge catalyst to our friendship.

Second, because of our proximity, we knew where each other was "winning" and what challenges we were facing both at work and at home. When you're literally this close to each other, you know what time the person sitting at the desk across from you called home to say, "I'm on my way ..." and what time he actually left to go home. There really are few secrets. Through the course of a day, topics of conversation will range from how the Big Idea for this weekend's celebration service is developing to what latest trick your newborn is doing, to what happened on *American Idol* the night before.

Finally, because of our proximity, we developed a strong trust between us — and the soft stuff of trust is what helps partnerships and teams to maximize their potential. This is huge. I know Eric has my back. He would do just about anything for me, and he often does. I also know that as passionate as he is about the arts, he is more passionate about the church and people experiencing real, biblical community. For Eric, good art and the development of great artists are ultimately means to an end, and that end is help-ing people find their way back to God. We have a partnership that I wouldn't trade for anything.

PARAMETERS

Planning and proximity have definitely helped Dave and Eric to become good friends and partners; but most important, these two key players have the same parameters for accomplishing the mission to which God has called CCC. Week after week they have to make decisions regarding songs, scripts, videos, and any number of other creative elements, and these stated parameters are what give them a basis on which to dialogue when making tough choices. At CCC, the primary parameter is our mission: helping people find their way back to God. Our strategy to accomplish this mission involves the three experiences of celebrating, connecting, and contributing weekly. However, when it comes to the particulars of making tough decisions about a specific song, video, dance, live theater moment, and so on, we need something more. The two questions that we have found helpful are these:

1. **Does this creative element help us accomplish the Big Idea?**
2. **Does this creative element distract from the Big Idea?**

For us to say yes to a creative element, we have to answer yes to question 1 and no to question 2. Otherwise, we don't use that element.

Here's what Eric has to say about the value of these two questions that serve as parameters for us:

> The word "distract" in question 2 is critical. For example, a few years ago I would have said that doing a song by Madonna would distract from the Big Idea. Just a few years ago, she was a cultural icon for sex — *Erotica* was the title of one of her CDs. But now she's pursuing a "spiritual path," and she's married and the mother of two children. So last year, someone in a Big Idea meeting suggested a song she recorded — "More" from the *Dick Tracy* soundtrack. We performed it at our weekend celebration services because when we put it to the test of these two questions, we answered, "Yes, this creative element does help us accomplish the

Big Idea," and "No, this creative element does not distract from the Big Idea." Now, on the flip side, even if her hit song "Papa Don't Preach" would have fit the Big Idea in 1996, we wouldn't have performed it because too many people would have responded in one of two ways: Either (1) "Wow, I can't believe they're performing a Madonna song. I'm offended!" Or (2) "Wow, I can't believe they're performing a Madonna song. How cool!" Here's the catch: both responses would have distracted from the Big Idea. The Big Idea never sends the message, "Look how cool we are," or "Let us shock you with this art." The Big Idea is that week's theme or topic, and ultimately it's all focused toward helping people find their way back to God.

The two questions remind me of a study I once read that examined children's playground behavior. In the study, two very similar playgrounds were built with comparable equipment. The only difference was that one was fenced in, and the other was not. The study found that the children who played on the fenced-in playground roamed freely, seemed to have fun, and overall got along quite well.

In contrast, the children on the playground with no boundaries used very little of the equipment, often huddled together, and appeared to be much more agitated with one another. Our two questions are the fence around the playground for Eric and Dave. They agreed on these questions several years ago, and they have proved to be extremely helpful in making tough calls as well as in relationally navigating through what could be very rough waters.

BACK TO THE DINING ROOM

How did the story at the beginning of this chapter, about the play titled *The Dining Room*, conclude? Eric and Dave met one-on-one to discuss the profanity in the script. After some debate, they agreed to leave it in, with Eric making some minor adjustments where doing so wouldn't take away from the impact and the genuine expression of feelings on the part of the characters in the play. They both agreed that the Big Idea in this case was for CCC to present outstanding art that would give our people an opportunity to bring their friends and possibly introduce them to the church for the very first time. Since the play wasn't being presented in a weekend celebration service, the profanity didn't seem to distract from the Big Idea. The family members portrayed in the play weren't claiming to be Christ followers, and eliminating the profanity actually may have been detrimental to the show.

Eric followed Dave's advice regarding the ending of the script. The last scene was a coming together of the family around the table to share a meal. All of the food in the show was pantomimed, so no "real" food was on display. Dave suggested that the family take Communion. Eric still describes the idea as "brilliant." They didn't have to change a line. The family simply pantomimed passing the bread and wine around the table and celebrating Jesus — no, they didn't say "Jesus," but that didn't mean they weren't celebrating him. It was a profound way to conclude the show and communicate in a powerful way that in spite of all the brokenness and dysfunction we may experience, in the end we can always come back to Jesus.

Dave and Eric are the two most important players in creating our Big Idea. The *Dining Room* story is one of many examples of how their relationship is built on trust and risk.

CHAPTER 9

THE BIG IDEA CREATIVE TEAM MEETING

It's one thing to read about, think about, and talk about creating multiple weekly experiences that align to create one Big Idea that communicates itself across all age groups and in large groups as well as small groups. Of course, it's another thing to go ahead and do it. This chapter provides you with pointers on how to have a successful Big Idea creative team meeting — how to walk out of this meeting every week with a beginning, middle, and end of a service that will happen nine weeks from now.

The first thing we have to deal with is the mistaken notion that "creative" and "meeting" cannot be used in the same sentence. I know that most artist types can't stand being held down in a meeting for more than, say, five minutes. But whether they like to admit it or not, artists need some boundaries; they need a border on the canvas upon

> The first thing we have to deal with is the mistaken notion that "creative" and "meeting" cannot be used in the same sentence.

which they will work. Many times churches leave artists to their own devices. Pastors tell their creative arts types, "Just come up with something, and let me know what it is by the end of the week." Well, in many cases you've just perfected the fine art of encouraging procrastination — because that arts director will hem and haw and think and wait and wait and think and end up at three in the morning on Sunday putting together a song list and then barely communicating it to his or her teams before the first service.

Remember the study mentioned in chapter 8 about the kids at two different playgrounds — one with a fence and one without? The borders of the fenced-in playground had been defined, and as a result, the children played more freely. Artists are like that too, and enforcing a discipline that says, "We are going to meet here once a week for two hours and walk out of this room with a completed worship service," gives your artists the parameters they need to create great art and to do so efficiently.

This discipline will take some getting used to, though. Whenever you begin brainstorming in this manner, make sure you give the process time to sink in before you make major adjustments to the flow. Ritual plays a big part in the comfort levels of your artists, so the implementation of the Big Idea should not be characterized by a constant altering of the formula. Find a groove and stick with it — then after a few months, you can take a look at the flow and see what might be fine-tuned to better cater to your creative needs.

So let's start at the very beginning, which, ironically, is not the actual start of the meeting. The lead pastor and creative arts director will need to think through many details before the meeting actually begins. Here's how to prepare.

BEFORE

To start planning nine weeks in advance, you need to be able to accurately assess what it is you actually do in your services. This is the "know thyself" portion of the preparation. Many churches have prescribed formats for their services — liturgies that have been passed down through the ages and that have shaped the worship services we now know and love (or would love to change). For some of us, there were no liturgies to draw from, and we were left defining our model or template on our own.

Many times this template formation happens naturally, as a church begins to define itself and its ethos through the material it presents and, more important for us now, through the order in which it presents the material. Eric likes to call this order of events the *skeleton* of our service. I like that metaphor because it allows the order to be defined as needing layers on top of it — the *skin*, if you will. If you come to a Community Christian Church celebration service, you may not see the skeleton, because we are constantly mixing it up and changing things. But underneath the skin of the Big Idea and a constantly evolving worship experience is a skeleton that we adhere to, for the most part, on a week-to-week basis. Following is the skeleton for our adult weekend services. (Remember, this is just us; replace the nouns you see with words that describe your own church's style, system, and mode.)

1. Praise choruses (opening of service)
2. Campus pastor moment (greeting)
3. Creative element (video, sketch, or song or a combination)
4. Teaching
5. Communion
6. Giving back to God (offering)
7. Praise choruses (closing of service)

In this skeleton, all of the praise choruses will be lyrically linked to the Big Idea for reinforcement, and oftentimes the creative element will be a combination of elements. The creative element could be moved to after the teaching time to provide resolution rather than set up the message.

You must define for yourself, your staff, and your church the elements of your preferred skeleton. Once you have figured out what those elements are, grab about ten or twelve half sheets of paper.

Write the name of each element that you have identified as part of your skeleton on one half sheet, with room for additional notes below. For example, CCC's pages might look like this:

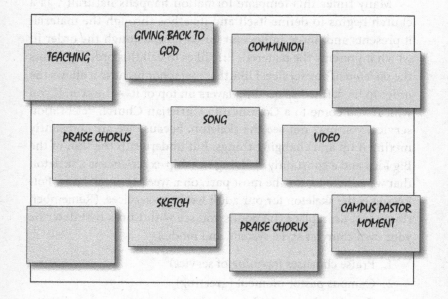

You will bring these sheets of paper to your Big Idea creative arts meeting, and they will be the tools used to craft your service,

> You must define for yourself, your staff, and your church the elements of your preferred skeleton.

not only the content, but the order in which these elements appear. Don't forget to include a few blanks; you never know what kinds of things you might dream up, and what different elements you'll want to add to your skeleton that week. Since these are templates you'll want to bring every week, it's a good idea to use a computer to print out some of your most regularly used skeleton elements.

To make best use of the tools presented here, view each of your skeleton elements as "most likely used," not "must be used." Think of these sheets of paper as items you have in your hip pocket, waiting and ready to be distributed. Often in our meetings, we won't pass around the sheets until the last half hour, trying to keep the brainstorming alive and kicking as long as possible before committing it to paper. Once you've started moving the sheets around and working on the order of the service, you'll have difficulty continuing to think of possible new ideas that might challenge the framework already established. So bring the tools, but don't use them too early!

As you analyze your services and the facts that make them successful and repeatable, you may realize that some parts of the service take more time to develop and brainstorm than others. Obviously, teaching fits into this category. At nine weeks out, the teaching team may have an inkling of where they want to take the message, but a manuscript complete with a bullet point outline may still be a few weeks away. That's why the teaching team at CCC completes the manuscript *after* the Big Idea creative arts meeting, not *during*. I am thinking about and mulling over and marinating the content of our messages long before I otherwise would if I were not part of this meeting and part of the arts team.

So if teaching is something that needs to be brainstormed and developed *after* the Big Idea meeting, the next analysis of your skeleton should determine whether any elements need to be, or would benefit from being, brainstormed *before* the meeting. For CCC, two elements fit into this category.

Pre-Brainstorm Brainstorms
A foundational part of our skeleton is the performance of "pop songs," songs found in the culture that have potential spiritual significance and connection to the Big Idea. However, one could spend probably two hours each week just listening to the many songs that might work for any given week or any given topic. Taking time in

the Big Idea meeting to listen to and evaluate each song would not be particularly efficient. So we hold a separate brainstorming meeting once a month just to listen to music, and we bring in artists whose expertise is in music to help us listen to and select songs for each week. These brainstorming sessions happen prior to the Big Idea creative team meeting; at that meeting, one representative brings to the table the two or three "best picks" from the previous brainstorming session.

Similarly, CCC has a creative writing team that gathers once a month to brainstorm ideas for sketches, videos, and all sorts of creative arts ideas that, once decided upon, would need to be written. Again, once those ideas are honed into a couple of "winners," they are brought to the Big Idea meeting by one representative.

> Brainstorming sessions happen prior to the Big Idea creative team meeting with one representative bringing to the table the two or three "best picks" from the previous brainstorming session.

These pre-brainstorm brainstorms are critical for team development in the particular areas that your church's service skeleton depends on each week. However, after you examine your skeleton and look at the size of your creative team, you may decide it's premature to launch pre-brainstorm meetings. Once you begin brainstorming on a week-to-week basis following the Big Idea format, you will need to monitor the meeting and ask yourself, "Is a part of this meeting dominating the conversation at the expense of other elements?" "Could we be more efficient if we had a pre-brainstorm brainstorm?" The dominating element may be special music, as it is for CCC, or it may be something completely different. Your skeleton will determine what it is, and you'll find it very advantageous to be aware of it and make adjustments as necessary.

Who Needs to Play?

The last step before commencing your first Big Idea creative team meeting is to decide who needs to be there. This decision can have tremendous ramifications, so take it seriously. Probably more people than are needed will desire to attend the meeting and influence the direction of your weekend services. Having an "open room" may prove detrimental over time to the rhythm of your meetings. Many times, people use this kind of meeting as a platform to advocate the kinds of ideas they think their church needs to do "more of." What started out as a creative meeting ends up becoming a political mess of "what we should be doing" versus "what we are doing" and "what we shouldn't be doing."

The best advice we can give you is this: First, remember that it's a lot easier to invite additional help than it is to "un-invite" unwanted help. Second, be selective in terms of the people you bring into the meeting. These people need to be able to think creatively but also need to be able to have their ideas bypassed from time to time. Our motto has always been that the best idea wins no matter who thought of it. And egos, to paraphrase Quincy Jones, need to be checked at the door in this kind of endeavor. One of our arts directors, Greg Eichelberger, says, "When I arrive, I need to come prepared with my ideas, but with an open mind. I love how we are able to bounce around ideas without anyone needing their idea to be the one we pick."

> Our motto has always been that the best idea wins no matter who thought of it.

When we first began these meetings, five of us were present: Eric, our creative arts director; our music minister; two volunteers who had experience in brainstorming and theater arts; and me. That group formed the foundation of healthy brainstorming in which an idea is simply that — an idea — and in which everything is emotionally invested but nothing is personally invested, so that when an idea falls flat on its face, the person who said it out loud isn't indicted or punished. The development of a healthy brainstorming culture is important and needs to take place in an "agenda-less" room.

Make a list of "possible suspects" who might attend or already attend your creative team meeting. Consult with others on staff about the dynamics of the group, and determine the key people you need to invite. If you're hesitant to ask certain people, even if most signs are positive, you might want to consider waiting to invite them.

DURING

You're ready with your team assembled and the bell sounds. Now what?

Here is how our church shapes its Big Idea creative team meeting; we hope you'll find it helpful to read about how we do it. But please know that while the principles may be something to emulate, the last thing you want to do is adopt a "cookie cutter" approach and fit your format into a prescribed mold. This is not "cut and paste" Church Services 101. You will need to take this information and shape it to fit your church's skeleton and ethos. This is what works for us; we hope it will be useful to you and your team as well.

> This is not "cut and paste" Church Services 101.

Prayer

We begin our meeting with — you guessed it — prayer. The very start of the meeting is the perfect opportunity to call upon the Creator of all living things. Being able to join God on his mission and to create services that will help people find their way back to him is a high privilege. Never take it for granted, and call upon his power and creativity early and often. Got it? Good.

The Graph

The meeting then turns to the content of the day. Nine weeks from now, we'll be communicating this message to our congregations, so the teaching team representative, in our case Tim Sutherland, describes for us the heart of the Big Idea graphs that he and his team composed weeks earlier. Then everyone has a chance to ask questions regarding this Big Idea: "Do any doctrinal questions need to be addressed?" "How does this weekend in the series differ from the next weekend or last weekend?" "What truths should people take away from the service?" CCC is a nondenominational church with many different participants in the Big Idea creative team meeting, including those from a wide range of churched and unchurched backgrounds. Often some of us need clarification just to sort through the previous baggage we bring with us. Since many of those who attend CCC have similar baggage, asking these questions helps us delve into the hearts and minds of the people we are most passionate to reach.

Open-Forum Brainstorming

After all issues needing clarification have been addressed, we begin a time of open-forum brainstorming. This forum allows team members to express their ideas regarding possible creative elements to be used in the service. Many times it's a movie, a song, or even a TV commercial; the point is to begin the process without automatically thinking, "How will this fit into a service?" We try to paint the first brainstorming session with as wide a brush as possible. Sometimes, of course, the brain is slow to move. That's when the occasional "near-topic" icebreaker can be helpful. Don't hesitate to bring out some icebreaker questions when the going is slow. Here are a few that Eric pulls out when needed:

1. "Finish this sentence: 'I recommend ...' Then tell us why."
   This exercise should prompt group members to think about

a recent book, movie, TV show, or music CD that they would recommend. It gets the group thinking creatively without the pressure of the Big Idea. When you go back to brainstorming, you have a whole set of new ideas.

2. "What is the biggest spectacle you've ever seen that is related to this topic?" The aim here is to find something that we've already censored out of our brainstorming because we think it's impossible to pull off in a church service.

3. "Give a rapid-fire, one-sentence summary of what you think the Big Idea is about, or of what it means to you." Compare the responses. This exercise forces people to make their brains and mouths start working and often is enough to get ideas flowing.

These questions will almost always get the group jump-started and moving in the right direction. Most of the time, a shortage of ideas is not the issue. The real problem is trying to pick from more ideas than we could ever use for one Big Idea.

Emergence of an Idea
Eventually someone will become passionate about one particular idea or another, and before you know it, two or more people are working out the details of some potentially amazing moment for the service. Let this idea breathe, even if it takes on some bizarre form that would never fit into your template or skeleton. Often the best ideas are shaped after the creative process has blown them out of proportion and then carved away the unnecessary portions to reveal a clear and sharp idea. So be careful not

> Often the best ideas are shaped after the creative process has blown them out of proportion and then carved away the unnecessary portions to reveal a clear and sharp idea.

to cut off an idea too fast with brainstorm killers such as "That'll never work," or "We could never pull that off." You may be absolutely right, but that doesn't mean the idea won't be the first step toward a truly great idea to enhance the Big Idea. Keep the dreaming going, and remember that you have nine whole weeks to put it together!

Emergence of the Order of Service
Sometime during the meeting we will introduce the song and sketch ideas pulled from the pre-brainstorm brainstorms, all the while listening to more ideas and music, and the worship leaders begin to put together worship songs that fit the topic. At this point the half sheets of paper come into play. We usually bring about ten permanent markers to the meeting so that many different players can compile the ideas and write them on the half sheets. That's when the fun really begins.

Since we are not bound by a specific liturgy that demands the same order of service every week, we lay out the half sheets on a table and consider the various elements, deciding on the best order. Often two very different songs will be competing for the same slot, and only as we determine the order of the service will a clear winner present itself. We at CCC have found the flexibility to shape the order of each service very advantageous, and even though we stick to our "skeleton" more times than not, this moment of possibility gives us the feeling of "new creation" every week.

AFTER

A few weeks after the Big Idea creative team meeting, the creative arts director and lead pastor should meet to discuss the progress of the Big Idea plans: What patterns (both good and bad) are developing, and how can the format be improved? But these leaders must be careful not to put their fingers in the wind every week and alter major components of the service in the name of "making adjustments." Artists need to know that their canvases aren't going to change color every week.

Once you've developed a rhythm of weekly meetings, you'll notice that many of your team members have found their "comfort zones" or "artistic bias," the patterns they prefer within the skeleton of your church's services. Some may begin to think you should use drama every week; others will think you should never write a sketch again. Some will start to think that video is the answer to every problem; others will think that this impersonal medium should be kept to a minimum. More often than not, these biases are linked directly to their areas of expertise or their art of choice, and every now and then you'll need to mix it up a little to keep them on their toes. Before long, they might start to "sanctify" these favorite elements and have difficulty seeing any reason why the service shouldn't include them every week — these elements have become almost holy to them. This is how the "church organ offering solo" came into existence and never seemed to leave many of our congregations — so watch for signs of "pseudo-sanctification"!

> Artists need to know that their canvases aren't going to change color every week.

One way to burst this bubble is to take one week to orchestrate an intentional veering from each member's area of expertise. Give the music people the job of brainstorming sketch ideas. Ask the theater types to develop "takeaways" for the teaching moments. Entrust your teaching pastors with the task of exploring video clip ideas. Fashion a quick mini-brainstorm and presentation time to gather these new ideas from very different places. This role switching will force team members to think differently about what they like and will allow them to see their art through someone else's eyes, an opportunity that can be very valuable. And when they come back to their comfort zone, the palette will be broader and more reflective, and they will be more trusting of others on the team with their favorite element. Tim Sutherland says of the experience, "In the

Big Idea meeting, I get ideas for Scripture and film clips and metaphors and images that I use regularly in what goes into our teaching that I wouldn't otherwise get. These ideas come from anybody and everybody in the Big Idea meeting, from the music guy, to the video person, to the interns serving in every imaginable capacity. No way would I have as many ideas as I do if it wasn't for the Big Idea meeting."

So now you know how to have your own Big Idea creative team meeting. Your next step is to have your own teaching team meeting. We'll tackle that endeavor in the next chapter.

CHAPTER 10

THE BIG IDEA TEACHING TEAM MEETING

"Hey, Timo!" That's how our collaborative team-teaching approach first got started.

From my very first weekend at Community Christian Church, before I prepared for a message, I would always make a long distance call to Tim Sutherland in Columbus, Ohio. Besides being a very good friend, Tim is also one of the smartest people on the planet! A typical phone call would go something like this (with the translation in parentheses):

Dave: Hey, Timo! *(Hi, Tim.)*

Tim: Yo! *(Hi, Dave.)*

Dave: Got a minute? *(I need some help with the message for this weekend.)*

Tim: Sure, what's up? *(What would this guy do without me?)*

Dave: We're starting a brand-new series called Things to Say before You Die, based on the last words of Jesus. And this week's Big Idea is "Forgive Them." *(That's all I have so far—please boot up your CD-ROM brain and download something for me.)*

Tim: Well, I was just reading Lewis Smedes's *Forgive and Forget*, and he says ..." *(I'd better get a really good Christmas gift this year!)*

And as we talked we would swap ideas, trade stories, exegete Scripture, and basically brainstorm my next message. Having scribbled down every idea, I would walk away from each phone call knowing two things for sure:

1. The content of this message is going to be a lot richer than if I had tried to come up with ideas on my own.
2. Not only is this message going to have better content, but I put it together in much less time than I could have if I were holed up by myself somewhere.

> Writing messages collaboratively is much more effective, but mostly it's a lot more fun!

After a couple of years of long-distance phone calls, Tim decided to move his family and his counseling practice to Chicago so he could be a part of Community Christian Church. And then those phone calls turned into lunch meetings or a few sets of tennis in the afternoon. But we always talked and collaborated on the upcoming message. Since that time, Tim has joined our staff and now leads the teaching team at CCC. And now I can't imagine writing a message on my own — partly because writing messages collaboratively is so much more effective, but mostly because it's a lot more fun!

ARE YOU A BASEBALL TEAM OR A BASKETBALL TEAM?

Before we get into the details of the teaching team meeting, we need to have a clear understanding of the kind of teaching team that best creates the Big Idea message. Almost all of the teaching teams that I have observed are like a baseball team with a pitching staff. That pitching staff will put one pitcher on the mound, and the whole crowd will watch to see if he can bring a victory to his team. A pitching staff always has a number one pitcher, called the ace. And if a big game is on the line, you always go with your ace to get the win.

The kind of teaching team that best creates the Big Idea is not like a pitching staff; it's more like a basketball team. All of the players on a basketball team have a position to play and know that if they are going to be successful, they have to pass the ball and run the play. A good basketball team must have all five players on the court and not just one pitcher on the mound. A basketball team will have a leading scorer, but to be a great team, every player must be able to shoot the ball and score. Our team at CCC is much more like a basketball team; we have some players who are more skilled for certain positions, but we depend on the entire team, not just one ace, for the victory.

> The kind of teaching team that best creates the Big Idea is not like a pitching staff; it's more like a basketball team.

Sometimes basketball teams are composed of highly recruited, drafted, and paid professionals. Other basketball teams are formed through pick-up games, and people draft each other. You show up at the playground or Y at a certain time of day because you know other guys will be there wanting to play, and you start a pick-up game. The teaching team that collaborates around a Big Idea to create a message can be a team composed of people who are all on staff at a megachurch, or it can be a pick-up team of pastors who love the teaching and agree to show up at the "playground" at the same time. This is not the kind of teaching-team approach that works only for a large church with a large staff. This is the kind of approach that any group of pastor-teachers (from churches small or large) could begin to implement today — if they understand that they are a basketball team and not a pitching staff.

THE TEACHING TEAM MEETING: THE FASTEST 105 MINUTES OF YOUR WEEK!

What if I told you that you would never again spend more than 105 minutes a week to come up with a text, an introduction, an outline, and a conclusion with solid application for your message? Would you be interested? If you do any teaching, you would be. We do it every week! I know 105 minutes sounds quick — it is. But we don't cut corners; 105 minutes is really all the time our teaching team needs. Now, most pastors spend much more time than that just deciding what to talk about, but we already took care of that when we laid out our one-year Big Idea plan. So how do we get all that preparation done in only 105 minutes? Hold on ...

> To come up with a text, an introduction, an outline, and a conclusion with solid application, 105 minutes is really all the time our teaching team needs.

Focus (5 minutes)

During the focus time, we hand out and review the Big Idea graphs and the Big Idea celebration service summary. The Big Idea graphs give our team of teachers a quick overview of the Big Idea that emerged in our one-year Big Idea planning meeting. The Big Idea celebration service summary reminds us of the creative elements we planned for this service at our Big Idea creative team meeting. The graphs keep us focused on one Big Idea, and the celebration service summary tells us where the teaching time fits into the overall service. While a handful of us in the room review these handouts, those who are collaborating with us via teleconferencing or video conferencing are able to look at the copies that were emailed to them. Whether team members are in the room or thousands of miles away, Tim gives us a rundown of the Big Idea to make sure everyone on the team is focused.

Desired Outcomes (10 minutes): Head, Heart, and Hands

"Beginning with the end in mind" is an important aspect of the teaching team meeting. Tim asks us to clarify precisely what we want to accomplish with this Big Idea teaching time. This might seem redundant after all of the previous discussions of this Big Idea, but it's critical that we all understand what we are challenging people to live out. Usually these desired outcomes can be understood in terms of "head," "heart," and "hands."

- *Head*. How do we want people to think differently?
- *Heart*. How do we want people to feel differently?
- *Hands*. How do we want people to act differently?

Here are a couple of other questions we ask to get at the desired outcomes: "What do you want to be different in the life of the person who experiences this Big Idea?" "When people walk out the doors after experiencing the Big Idea, how will they be changed?" As we answer these questions and become clear about our desired outcomes, we write them on giant sticky notes. We keep these desired outcomes in front of the whole team so we are focused on the change we want to see happen.

> "Beginning with the end in mind" is an important aspect of the teaching team meeting.

Brainstorming (45 minutes)

If clarifying the desired outcomes is the most important part of the teaching team meeting, brainstorming ideas for the message is the most fun. It's during the brainstorming that we really see the benefit of the team. You can try to brainstorm by yourself, but you're really just talking to yourself. When you have a team of people who are thinking creatively together, and one person reaches his or her limit on an idea, another person's creativity and experience can take the idea to the next level. That's why a team of people brainstorming will always develop an idea to a more profound level than an individual thinking alone. So when we begin brainstorming, anything goes!

> When you have a team of people who are thinking creatively together, and one person reaches his or her limit on an idea, another person's creativity and experience can take the idea to the next level.

The most successful teaching team brainstorming sessions happen when all of us come prepared and all Tim has to say is, "Okay, what do you have?" and we are off and running with stories, Scriptures, illustrations, insights, props, and jokes and jotting more ideas on the oversize sticky notes than we will ever use! However, as with all teams, some days we need more coaching than others. Here are a few ways to jump-start the brainstorming on those days:

- *Hot potato.* Bring a ball to the teaching team meeting. The first person to catch the ball has to come up with a new angle on the Big Idea within fifteen seconds. After they offer their contribution, they toss the ball to another team member, who has fifteen seconds to come up with another angle.

- *Debate.* Divide the teaching team into two sides and have each side argue a position regarding the Big Idea. Give each side a chance to argue and respond, and when the debate begins to lose momentum, have the sides switch and argue the other position. With a competitive group, this exercise can get the juices flowing and stimulate team members to think differently.

- *Beg, borrow, or steal.* Download a manuscript from two or three other teachers and review what they have done with this topic or text and critique how they did. If the teachers are gifted, you will almost always discover a few good ideas that you can incorporate into your teaching. If you seem to have a shortage of good ideas, this exercise will get the brainstorming moving in the right direction.

Tons of other ideas for facilitating brainstorming sessions are available in books and online. Just keep it fresh and keep it moving.

Structure (30 minutes)

Because we like the brainstorming part of the meeting so much, we'll often have a team member keep time so that we know when 60 of our 105 minutes are up. Then we have to discipline ourselves to begin to put all of this creativity into some kind of structure. If we are doing expository teaching, then we will work through the text in the Bible and lay out a verse-by-verse structure that allows the Scripture to speak to the listener. Most of our teaching is topical, and then we rely on several different structures to best communicate God's truth. Here are a few of the structures we use:

- *Narrative.* A narrative message will be structured like acts in a play. If the message is a three-act play, then the problem or issue will be revealed in act 1, the problem will intensify and reach a crisis in act 2, and the problem will reach a resolution in act 3. This kind of structure is great for creating memorable experiences and inspiring listeners through powerful storytelling.

- *Problem-solution.* This simple structure can be put into place in a couple of ways. One way is to introduce the problem, analyze it, and finally provide a solution. The other way is to introduce the problem, offer possible solutions, and conclude by presenting Jesus as the real solution. This kind of structure works well for persuading listeners and presenting an apologetic.

- *Question-answer.* When you structure a topical message in this way, you can do it with (1) one question and one answer, (2) multiple questions and multiple answers, or (3) one question with multiple wrong answers and one correct answer (my preferred pattern). This type of teaching pattern is helpful for informing and helping listeners make a decision.

- *Not this, but that.* A message structured in this way yields many of the same results as the problem-solution pattern, but I find it more interesting. Typically you present the problem, then provide a series of faulty solutions, and finally conclude with the correct solution. In other words, you structure your message so that you are saying, "It's not this ... And it's not this ... But it is this."

- *Ambiguity-clarity.* Many topics (the problem of pain, the role of angels, etc.) tend to be less than clear. The ambiguity-clarity structure allows you to state the ambiguity in Scripture and in life and then give the best explanation from Scripture and experience. This structure is effective because it moves people forward in their spiritual journey by increasing their understanding of tough topics while acknowledging that there is still mystery.

- *What? So what? Now what?* This is our team's favorite structure. It asks three simple questions about the Big Idea that we are teaching: (1) What are we talking about? (2) So what makes this so important that people have to hear this? (3) Now what do we want them to do as a result of hearing this Big Idea? What this structure does best is make sure that our teaching is oriented toward life application.

This is the place where teams are most likely to get stuck. And if you get stuck and fail to create a structure, you will not be able to take the next step. So what do you do? Whenever we get stuck at this point in the process, one team member (and you never know who) will point his finger like a gun at another person on the team and ask, "If you had to preach this right now, how would you do it?" (In other words, "If your life depended on your delivering this talk right now, what would you say?") It's extreme, but we always come up with a structure.

> Whenever we get stuck, one team member will point his finger like a gun at another person on the team and ask, "If you had to preach this right now, how would you do it?"

Consensus (10 minutes)

Our 105 minutes are almost up, so we use the last fifteen minutes to make sure we are ready to move forward as a team. In the first ten minutes, we review the content and structure and make sure that everyone on the team can live with it. You may think ten minutes isn't enough time to reach a consensus; I can only tell you that our experience has been that we now trust the team and the process more than any one of us trusts him- or herself. We reach consensus when we review the content and structure of the message and everyone says, "I'm okay." Once we get the okay from everyone in the room, on the telephone, and online, we are ready to "divvy."

Divvy Time (5 minutes)

During the last five minutes of the teaching team meeting, Tim asks everyone in the room which part of the message they would most like to write up. As people volunteer to author various sections, Tim writes their initials next to those parts of the structured outline on the giant sticky notes on the wall. Sometimes all of us get the section we want, and sometimes we don't. But again, we all trust the process and the team more than we trust ourselves.

NEXT STEPS: WHAT HAPPENS ONCE THE 105 MINUTES HAVE EXPIRED?

The 105 minutes have run out. What happens next is truly an amazing blend of low-tech and high-tech collaboration in what I believe is the best way to create Big Idea teaching.

Teaching Team Notes with Assignments

Within twenty-four hours Tim collects all of the notes on the giant sticky notes and types up what we call teaching team notes. These notes include references to stories we might want to use or books for further research or links to websites mentioned in the teaching team meeting. This document is normally no more than one page but is an important guide as we take the next step in producing a teaching manuscript. The teaching team notes are emailed to all members of the teaching team along with a designation regarding which section each person agreed to do. All of us know that we need to email our assigned sections to Tim seventeen days in advance of the first weekend that the message is taught. In our case, we all know that we have an assignment due by 5:00 p.m. on Wednesday.

1.0

Once we all get our assignments to Tim, he has about twenty-four hours to edit the manuscript and produce what we call the 1.0. The 1.0 is the first complete version of a word-for-word manuscript for the Big Idea. The brilliant part of this process is that the 1.0 arrives in my email sixteen days before I have to teach on that Big Idea. Imagine having a completed manuscript that is truly yours sixteen days before you have to teach. It is awesome!

2.0, 3.0, 4.0 ... Final!

With the 1.0 "in the can," you have time to live with it and apply it to your own life. You have more than two weeks to make it even better — and that's what always happens. To my knowledge we have never taught from a 1.0 manuscript, but we could. For the next sixteen days emails fly back and forth among the teaching team members as we swap new and improved edits of the 1.0. You might get a 2.0 edit that includes a joke you "just have to use." And then a 3.0 that eliminates a section that seemed repetitive. A few days later comes a 4.0 with a better conclusion. And then you might receive a 5.0 with minor changes that improve the flow. This part of the collaborative process is totally free-form and spontaneous, and it works! And all along the way, you've had total involvement as part of a team.

THE TEACHING TEAM: WHAT YOU CAN'T SEE THAT MAKES IT WORK

About every week people sit in on our Big Idea creative team meeting or our Big Idea teaching team meeting so they can observe the collaborative process in action. They see a young and very creative group of people from a variety of artistic backgrounds all thinking creatively about one Big Idea. They see the use of technology such as teleconferencing, video conferencing, and online chat rooms to develop the Big Idea. And they see leaders who are prepared with the right handouts and resources to maximize our meeting time. When they leave, they've seen a lot of cool stuff, but I believe it is what they can't see that makes the teaching team really work.

> It is what you can't see that makes the teaching team really work.

Teamwork

The concept of a teaching team is not really a new concept. Over the last fifteen years, many megachurches have moved toward the baseball style of teaching team that uses teachers like a pitching rotation. Historically, the larger Roman Catholic parishes have long employed this kind of teaching team. When you came to Mass, you didn't know who was going to give the homily, and quite frankly, it didn't matter, because you were there for the Mass.

The Big Idea teaching team is more like a team of teachers than a teaching team. This team is like a basketball team in that the members depend on each other every play of every game. If one person doesn't run the play, the whole play breaks down. Consequently, trust is a huge unseen component that makes this team work. We trust each other to show up prepared. We trust each other to do our best writing. We trust each other to share our new ideas after the 1.0 is finished. We totally trust that all members of the team are giving their best. Trust and teamwork make this team of teachers the best it can be.

> Trust and teamwork make this team of teachers the best it can be.

Absence of Ego
I don't know if you can say that you are ego-less and still be ego-less. (It's like saying you are humble — the second you say it, you cease to be it.) But I don't know how else to describe our Big Idea teaching team other than to say that it is a team without big egos. You can't see it, but it's evident during the 105 minutes when the idea that wins the day and sets the direction comes from a visitor rather than the person with the most seniority. The absence of ego is also evident in front of the congregation when the teacher references the work that the teaching team did rather than the work that he or she did. It's evident after a celebration service when any one of us hears, "Oh, you are my favorite," and we respond with, "Oh, thanks, but we're a team." Andrew Carnegie said, "You can accomplish whatever you want as long as you don't care who gets the credit." It's not about the individual teacher, and that's what makes this team of teachers work!

Leadership
We've always had one person take the lead on the Big Idea teaching team. When we started this collaborative approach, I ran the point.

For the last several years, Tim Sutherland has provided leadership. Having a point person who is responsible for getting the product where it needs to be, when it needs to be there, has been invaluable. The teaching team is like an orchestra: if we didn't have a conductor, no one would know when to come in and when to crescendo. The leader of the teaching team makes sure all members of the team know their roles: what sections they're writing, how long each section should be, when they're due, and so on. To the outside observer, the team may seem to function without a leader, but that's not the case. Having someone who provides leadership and coaches the team is essential for victory.

> Having a point person on the teaching team who is responsible for getting the product where it needs to be, when it needs to be there, has been invaluable.

Adaptability

During the last eight years we've had a variety of teachers on our team. Some teachers prefer a narrative style, some prefer three points and a conclusion, and others would like to avoid any structure at all. Some like to teach from a manuscript, others from notes, and still others from no notes at all. Despite the variety of preferences and styles, our team has been able to create a teaching product that is adaptable and effective for all. Here are a few reasons why:

- *Word-for-word manuscript.* The 1.0 manuscript is usually about a twenty-page-long document featuring 18-point Times New Roman type and 1.5 line spacing. The 1.0 always has more content than will be needed and therefore is longer than the final. Because the 1.0 is a manuscript, a teacher who wants to teach from an outline can easily put it into outline form. The person who prefers no notes can simply memorize the notes and leave them behind when it's time to teach.

- *Ownership*. All of the teachers are involved in the process and have ownership of the teaching from the beginning when they pick out the Big Ideas one year in advance, to the 105-minute meeting when they help create the manuscript by writing part of the 1.0. This level of ownership gives each teacher buy-in at every step of the process so that the finished manuscript is something they created and not something forced on them.
- *Finish lines*. With a finish line sixteen days before you'll have to stand in front of the congregation, you can relax knowing that you have plenty of time to adapt the manuscript. If you want to give a narrative message more structure, you can. If you want to give it a memorable refrain, you can. Most pastors don't finish their messages until Friday or Saturday, but the sixteen-day-out finish line gives you ample time to adapt the manuscript to your style.

Discipline

Our ethic of entrepreneurship along with a culture of discipline is something you don't see from a distance. But our relentless determination to constantly create new things while at the same time planning well in advance has served our teaching team well. If we skipped the 105-minute meeting whenever something else came up, the Big Idea process wouldn't work. If one team member decided not to email his or her

> Relentless determination to constantly create new things while at the same time planning well in advance has served our teaching team well.

section in by 5:00 p.m. on Wednesday, it wouldn't work. If we didn't finish the 1.0 until the Saturday morning before it had to be taught that night, it wouldn't work. The discipline of crossing these finish lines on time plays a major role in the success of our team of teachers.

THE CHALLENGES OF A TEACHING TEAM

"What about my own style of teaching?" "Who gets to make the final call?" "Isn't it confusing to be working on several different teachings at once?" Those are great questions — the kind of questions that must be asked and answered before you join a team of teachers. Here are the three biggies:

Biggy Question 1: Are You Willing to Trust a Team More Than Yourself?

I love running. I like golf. And I like tennis. But my favorite sport is basketball. The difference between running, golf, tennis, and basketball is that only basketball is a team sport. Depending on your own running ability for which place you come in is completely different from being a part of a team where you count on the other players and they count on you to bring the victory. Team teaching is a team sport. The good news is that the success of your team doesn't depend completely on you. And the bad news is that it doesn't depend completely on you. You have to be willing to trust the team more than you trust yourself. If you can answer yes to this question, then you might be ready for a teaching team.

> You have to be willing to trust the team more than you trust yourself.

Biggy Question 2: Can You Multitask?

Before you say yes to the question, "Can you multitask?" let me explain what you are saying yes to. When you join up with the Big Idea teaching team, you are saying yes to working on three different teachings all of the time. Let's count 'em: there's the teaching that you will discuss at the 105-minute meeting for which you are preparing; there's the teaching assignment that you agreed to write that is due this week; and there's the teaching that you will give this weekend as you continue to fine-tune the 1.0 until it becomes the final manuscript. Are you willing and able to say yes to that kind of multitasking? If not, you should stick to preparing messages on your own.

Biggy Question 3: Are You Willing to Change Your Style?

Everyone has a unique style, and while the Big Idea manuscript is very adaptable, the truth is, your style will change. You will be influenced tremendously by the other teachers and will never teach exactly the same way again. Now, I strongly believe that this change will be for the better, but you should know up front that if you say yes to a teaching team, you are also saying, "I'm willing to change my teaching style."

Can you say yes to these three biggies? Before you decide, let me describe just a few of the many benefits of the Big Idea team-teaching approach.

THE BENEFITS OF A TEACHING TEAM

I intentionally saved this section for the end of the chapter so I could sell you on the idea of the Big Idea teaching team. I knew if I wrote about the benefits at the beginning, the reasons for being part of such a team would be so obvious to me that the rest of the chapter would be meaningless. Here is why you should join a teaching team ...

Ready?

It's better — it's simply better in almost every way! I've been a pastor for the last sixteen years, and I grew up in the home of a pastor. My brother is a pastor; two of my

> Here is why you should join a teaching team: it's simply better in almost every way!

uncles are pastors. I know the gig. And I'm telling you that being part of a team is so much better than doing it on your own.

Still not sure? Let me explain the benefits:

Better Theology

The theology of any church is almost always going to be better and richer when there is a teaching team, because no one person can offer the fullness of interpretation that emerges in a solid community of theologically gifted leaders and teachers. Stanley Hauerwas explains this concept in *Unleashing the Scripture*: "Scripture can be interpreted only in the context of an interpretive community. Strategies of interpretation are not those of an independent agent facing an independent autonomous text, but those of an interpretive community of which the reader is but a member."[1] Interpretation of Scripture, like every other function of the church, is meant to be done in community, because we are relational creatures serving a relational God.

Better Content

I remember the days before we had the Big Idea teaching team in place, and I'm now living in the days with a great team of teachers. Our teaching today includes much better content, yet I spend half as much time in preparation as I once did — ten hours a week compared to twenty hours a week. How can the content be better when I'm investing less time? Our team of teachers includes teachers from at least five different churches all working on the same Big Idea. Many more man-hours are spent on one message, but fewer individual hours are spent on separate messages.

> Our teaching today has much better content, yet I spend half as much time in preparation as I once did.

Let's say that three churches have the potential of starting a Big Idea network. The choice those churches have is this: Will we spend twenty hours each to create three separate Big Ideas for a total of sixty hours, or will we spend ten hours each to create one Big Idea for a total of thirty hours? When you create a Big Idea network, you can develop better content by investing more network time and less individual time in one Big Idea.

Rob Bell compares preaching to cooking when he says, "Everything is better marinated."[2] When you finish the 1.0 sixteen days in advance, the content soaks deep into your life. The longer you get to live with the message, the more you can reflect on it, pray over it, and think through the specific application. A Big Idea message is not a shortcut; it's actually a "longcut." We spend more overall hours on one Big Idea teaching and get it done farther in advance, and the result is better content.

> "Everything is better marinated." When you finish the 1.0 sixteen days in advance, the content soaks deep into your life.

Better Illustrations

How many times have you had the right idea but have been unable to find an illustration to fit it? You might find yourself doing a Google search hoping to hit the jackpot. Or you might find yourself asking your spouse if the kids ever did anything funny related to that topic. You might even start digging through old messages, hoping that if you find something, no one will remember it. What you need in that moment is a roomful of people all brainstorming their favorite illustrations, stories, and personal anecdotes related to that idea. That's what you get when you are a part of a Big Idea team of teachers, and you end up with much better illustrations than if you were caged up in an office on your own.

I remember Fred Craddock, the master storyteller and godfather of preaching, saying, "You can't tell someone else's story." No contemporary has contributed more to the discipline of preaching than him. So it's with all due respect that I say, "I'm sorry Fred, but I think you're wrong." When you are in community with other teachers and are doing life together, you can tell each other's stories. It's not as if you're borrowing a story from Bill Hybels and inserting your wife's name where he said "Lynne." No, these are your friends, and you know them, their spouses, and their families. Many times I have told stories about Dave Richa, Brian Moll, Dave Dummitt, and other people on my teaching team. These aren't stolen stories from people I have only read about; these are stories from people with whom I work and with whom I do life! Bottom line, you get much better illustrations when a team is working on it than when you're on your own.

Better Use of Time

As I pointed out earlier, members of a teaching team get better content in half the time! And for me, being part of a team has freed up ten hours a week, allowing me to better use my gifts of leadership to move Community Christian Church forward and to advance the NewThing Network. This benefit of team teaching has been especially helpful to church planters. They are using this extra ten hours a week to develop emerging leaders and artists, a critical task for a start-up church.

When we started Community Christian Church, I spent many Saturday nights in a room all by myself, cramming to get ready for the next day. Why was I waiting until the last minute to prepare the teaching? It was either because I didn't have the time or because I didn't discipline the use of my time. Did you know that *Preaching Today* reports that most downloads of message manuscripts from its website happen on Saturday? Thankfully, I no longer face this kind of pressure. Now I'm always prepared with a manuscript completed sixteen days in advance.

> The Big Idea process means no more last-minute scrambling, which in turn means less stress, more sleep, and a real day off.

Not only does team teaching give you more time, but it also lends a better rhythm to the rest of your life. The Big Idea process means no more last-minute scrambling, which in turn means less stress, more sleep, and a real day off.

More Fun!

Finally, team teaching is a lot more fun than going it on your own. Sometimes people will come to a Big Idea meeting and observe the process, then comment, "Well, this works because you're all friends." Maybe. But I don't think it's the fact that we're friends that makes it work; I believe it's the work that makes us friends! I would never go back — never. Team teaching is just better. And not only is it better; it's also more fun!

CHAPTER 11

THE IMPLICIT BIG IDEA

I learned in grad school that there are at least two types of curriculum. One is explicit curriculum, and the second is implicit curriculum. In our church, our explicit curriculum is the Big Idea. You can't miss it. The Big Idea is the focus of brainstorming sessions months prior to its execution. The Big Idea is the subject of debate at teaching team meetings. The Big Idea is the concept behind a live theatrical moment. It's the catalyst for a campus pastor moment. It's the title of an adult small group discussion guide. It's the heart of a talk given by one of our Kids' City large group communicators. It's the theme of a man-on-the-street video interview produced by our Student Community team. The Big Idea is everywhere — from children to students to adults to senior citizens — and we're very intentional about keeping it that way.

Educators sometimes refer to implicit curriculum as "hidden curriculum." It's a less direct curriculum that speaks to the environment or context within which you are learning. It's not a curriculum that you find in print or as the topic of the Big Idea meeting. I'm not even sure we've ever tried to document it before. But this curriculum, while somewhat hidden, is no less pervasive or influential than the explicit Big Idea. It affects the arrangement of our desks in the offices. It impacts the

> This implicit curriculum is our culture, our ethos. It's how we go about developing the Big Idea.

order of the agenda for our staff meetings. It plays a significant role in our selection of personnel. This implicit curriculum is our culture, our ethos. It's how we go about developing the Big Idea.

How much this implicit curriculum preceded the development of the Big Idea process, and how much it is a by-product of the Big Idea, we're not sure. However, others have told us again and again that they realize its impact the moment they walk into one of our buildings, or have a conversation with a staff person, or sit in on one of our staff meetings. It's pretty much everywhere, and we're becoming increasingly intentional about keeping it that way. If our explicit curriculum is the Big Idea, then you might say that our implicit curriculum consists of several "secret ideas."

> If our explicit curriculum is the Big Idea, then you might say that our implicit curriculum consists of several "secret ideas."

SECRET IDEA 1: COLLABORATION

"Our ideas are always better than your idea. So get over it."

We hardly ever do anything alone. While I'm a teaching pastor, the thought of secluding myself in a quiet room for hours at a time to write a talk for a weekend celebration service without the help of my teammates is about as attractive as enduring a Chicago Bears loss to the Green Bay Packers (few things are worse!). Collaborative teams are a vital part of our implicit curriculum. They are what make us tick.

- A team of paid staff and dedicated volunteers *work together* to select the music for our weekend celebration services.
- A team of our NewThing teaching pastors as well as champions for our children's, students', and adults' ministries *join forces* every year to develop the Big Idea themes and series for the upcoming year.

- A team of staff and volunteers *work in partnership* to develop the Big Idea curriculum for our Kids' City ministry.

While we acknowledge that quiet time alone can be helpful and in many cases essential to creative productivity, for the most part we consider working by ourselves to be more like a punishment. In an interview with Leadership Network, Tom McGehee, author of *Whoosh: Business in the Fast Lane*, proposed the "road to collaboration."[1] He used the following words to describe this path:

Connection → Coordination → Cooperation → Collaboration

- *Connection: simply sharing information.* The very beginning of the road to collaboration is connection. For connection, I show up and let everyone know what's going on with me, and then everyone else tells me what's going on with them. Unfortunately, a lot of church staff meetings operate at this level. The staff members get along well and let each other know what's happening in their individual ministries. They may even enjoy spending time together, but often the road stops there.
- *Coordination: acting in concert with one another.* The purpose of coordination is to know what's going on around me so I know how it might affect me. It's mostly done to prevent problems rather than enable successes, but it's a step in the right direction. Coordination is what I would call a "prevent defense" approach to staff interaction. Everybody lets everybody else know what's happening so we can at least coordinate our calendars and *prevent* ministries from booking a similar event or activity at the same time.
- *Cooperation: looking out for one another.* Cooperation is more proactive than coordination. It's marked by the desire for mutual gain. The desire for collaboration usually prompts a

group or team to move to this level of interaction. When individuals are cooperating, a typical interaction may sound like this: "I know you're going to do this service project next week. Did you see this article in the paper about the community?" At the level of cooperation, people begin to look for ways to support each other and help each other be successful.

- *Collaboration: multiplying each other's strengths to produce a result that no one could achieve alone.* In collaboration we recognize potential success that none of us could achieve on our own, and we realize that the only way to experience this kind of success is to have everyone working together. I know that my success and the success of the team are dependent on our ability to work together, to team up, to form an alliance that seeks the best interests of everyone on the team. Not only does collaboration bring out the best a group collectively has to offer, but in the process of collaborating, the best an individual has to offer is brought to life.

In *Organizing Genius*, Warren Bennis refers to collaborative teams as "Great Groups." He writes:

> Great Groups think they are on a mission from God. Whether they are trying to get their candidate into the White House or trying to save the free world, Great Groups always believe that they are doing something vital, even holy. They are filled with believers, not doubters, and the metaphors that they use to describe their work are commonly those of war and religion. People in Great Groups often have the zeal of converts, people who have come only recently to see some great truth and follow it wherever it leads.[2]

We are on a mission from God — a mission to help people find their way back to God. We can't imagine a more compelling mission. It deserves not simply our individual best but our collective best, and for us, that means collaboration.

Collaborating like we do has many benefits:

1. *Collaboration reduces individual work.* We have already told you about the benefits of collaboration for our teaching team. Most pastors spend anywhere from eighteen to twenty-four hours preparing for a message, but through our collaborative approach, we've experienced at least a 50 percent reduction in preparation time. Our adult ministry team experiences the same kind of benefit when they collaborate to write the small group curriculum that is used at all of our locations rather than each location coming up with its own material. We experience this same benefit with our Student Community and Kids' City.

   > We are on a mission from God — a mission to help people find their way back to God. We can't imagine a more compelling mission. It deserves not simply our individual best but our collective best, and for us, that means collaboration.

2. *Collaboration recognizes people's individual contributions.* It's not uncommon for us to spend days or weeks developing a creative idea, and the person actually executing the idea may receive well-deserved accolades for a job well done. However, because of the collaborative work that went into developing the product, he or she is compelled to pass those affirmations on to the team and publicly express gratitude for the opportunity to work with such a great team.

3. *Collaboration reduces "star status" and results in less pressure on senior staff.* The Big Idea process is not dependent on a single "star" performer. To the contrary, the process doesn't work if it's all about one person. The very process stipulates

that a team effort will get the best possible results. At CCC our Big Idea is executed in many different locations, so we have numerous worship leaders, lead vocalists, actors, and teachers who "perform" before multiple audiences. The temptation to elevate any one person — worship leader, teacher, creative arts director, and so on — to "star status" is reduced significantly because so many people play so many different roles at so many different locations.

> The Big Idea process is not dependent on a single "star" performer. To the contrary, the process doesn't work if it's all about one person.

4. *Collaboration results in a better product.* Those who are willing to journey from connection to coordination to cooperation and ultimately to collaboration will get a better product. It will take some time and some chemistry, but the collaborative effort of the whole will be better than the single effort of each part. Through our NewThing Network we have multiple teams of people with a wide variety of talents, backgrounds, and experiences from all over the country contributing to the development of the Big Idea. For several years now, the result has been a much higher-quality product for all churches. Sure, each Big Idea still demands careful execution, but not only do many hands make light work — many hands make better work.

SECRET IDEA 2: HUMILITY

"Let me introduce you to the pastor's helper."

My brother, Jon, who has been at CCC with me from the start, told me about a time when he had lunch with one of our leaders at a local Mexican restaurant. He saw a woman he recognized from church. She seemed engaged in conversation, so he chose not to impose on her and settled for a smile and a quick wave. Just moments later, he looked up to see the woman and her friend standing near his table. Jon thought, "How nice — she wants to introduce her friend to her pastor." No sooner had that thought slipped through his head than he heard these words: "Let me introduce you to our pastor's helper." She was serious. She introduced Jon as the pastor's helper. Ouch! Humility may be a good thing, but her comment gave him an overdose, and too much of a good thing can leave you with an upset stomach. Nevertheless, it was a great reminder that a "founding pastor" to one person is simply a "helper" to another.

Jim Collins, in *Good to Great*, analyzed the histories of twenty-eight companies to determine the keys to long-term greatness. One of his researchers' findings was that the "great" companies were led by what he calls Level 5 leaders. He writes, "Level 5 leaders are a study in duality: modest and willful, humble and fearless." He illustrates the discovery like this:

HUMILITY + WILL = LEVEL 5

He continues:

> To quickly grasp this concept, think of the United States President Abraham Lincoln (one of the few Level 5 presidents in United States history) who never let his ego get in the way of his primary ambition for the larger cause of an enduring great nation. Yet those who mistook Mr. Lincoln's personal modesty, shy nature, and awkward manner as signs of weakness found themselves terribly mistaken, to the scale of 250,000 Confederate and 360,000 Union lives, including Lincoln's own.[3]

John the Baptist seems to have lived this same duality: modest and willful, humble and fearless. He said this about his successor, Jesus: "He must become greater; I must become less" (John 3:30). Yes, he was a humble man, but he also lived in the wild, ate locusts and honey, and, in the end, lived with such resolve that he gave up

> Your idea may have
> been the catalyst
> for a discussion or
> debate that resulted
> in the final idea that is
> implemented, but by the
> time that idea makes the
> final cut, no one except
> you will have any clue
> that it was actually your
> idea (or give a rip, for
> that matter).

his life for the cause of his successor, Jesus Christ.

Creating the Big Idea requires a high level of resolve and significant doses of humility. It often means that your idea will not make the cut. Because we're constantly in an environment where new ideas are being offered, criticized, modified, and overhauled, very rarely is any one person's original idea actually implemented. Your idea may have been the catalyst for a discussion or debate that resulted in the final idea that is implemented, but by the time that idea makes the final cut, no one except you will have any clue that it was actually your idea (or give a rip, for that matter). This aspect of the Big Idea process can be hard to take, but it causes all of us to hold on to our ideas rather loosely, knowing that the chances of one person getting credit for an idea are very slim. The Big Idea process fosters a culture of humility.

Those of us on the teaching team cringe at the temptation to compare teaching pastors. Every one of us has heard the mostly well-intended comment, "I really prefer your teaching style most," or "You're my favorite teacher." How do you respond to that? When you're working with a team as talented as the one I work with and experience the benefits of collaboration the way that we do, my gut-level response usually sounds something like this: "Thanks for your kind words. None of us do what we do on our own. We're a team." When I get an email from someone telling me how much my teaching has impacted them, I forward that email to the rest of the teams. Besides, we all know we couldn't do it without the other. As Pastor

Rick Warren says, "It's not about you." The Big Idea process helps us remember those words of wisdom.

In his book *Nine Things You Simply Must Do to Succeed in Love and Life,* Henry Cloud says:

> The roots of the word *humility* itself tell us something about these (successful) people. It comes from the root word *humus,* meaning "earth," and also from a Greek word that means "on the ground." The humble person has his feet on solid ground, not in la-la land. He is firmly planted in reality, and that reality includes his knowledge that he is a down-to-earth, gifted, but imperfect person just like everyone else. It is not lonely at the top if the top is on the bottom. There is a lot of good company to be had there — like the rest of the human race. The successful person has no need to be more than who he truly is. That is humility.[4]

SECRET IDEA 3: TRUST

"I know you won't let us down; we're banking on it."

There are several times in my weekly schedule when I know others are depending on me to come through for them, but few carry as much weight as 5:00 p.m. on Wednesday. Because we collaborate as a teaching team to develop the content for our weekend messages, we have specific finish lines (I sometimes think of them as "lifelines") we must cross in order to keep the collaborative process from breaking down. For our teaching team, 5:00 p.m. on Wednesday is when we need to have our weekly writing assignments turned in to our teaching team leader so that he can begin the process of pulling them together into one body of work that will speak powerfully to our congregations. But I'm not accountable only to the teaching team leader. Our teaching team includes pastors from five different states, representing a number of churches that include thousands of people. The section I write will be communicated to people in places all over the country. Sure, the Big Idea demands collaboration, but it also demands tremendous trust in your teammates, knowing that they will follow through on the commitments they make.

Maybe it's not good to have favorites, but I do. Dennis Taylor is one of my favorites. He is one of our volunteer producers. The reason I call him a volunteer is that he doesn't get paid, but he is a phenomenal producer. As a producer, Dennis is responsible for making sure that everyone arrives on time for the "cue-to-cue" prior to the service. He is also responsible for overseeing everything from lights to sound to media. Obviously, other people are running each of those areas, but at any given service, the Big Idea lives or dies based on the producer's ability to execute. One of the things I love about Dennis is his preservice huddle speech. Every time he produces, he offers a few words (sometimes a lot of words) to pump up the team before the service starts. My favorite part is when Dennis gives an extremely motivating talk that would rival Vince Lombardi's best locker room speech and then says, "Pastor Dave, what are you gonna talk about today?" I usually say, "Dennis you already preached. Let's get this service going." Dennis has a nine-to-five job. But he takes his weekend job no less seriously, maybe even more so, and he's great at it. One reason he's so good is that our creative arts staff members completely trust him to make it happen. With eight locations and more than twenty celebration services every week, we place tremendous trust in our staff and volunteer leaders to develop and execute the Big Idea.

SECRET IDEA 4: FUN

"If you want this much commitment, it had better be fun."

Southwest Airlines is famous for creating a fun work environment: "When you're having fun at work, it doesn't feel like work at all, it's better than tolerable, it's enjoyable. Having a job that's fun is certainly worth holding on to; people are more likely to accept ownership of their responsibilities, and much more inclined to go the extra mile to do whatever it takes."[5]

CCC is a fun place to work! When people ask me what I do for fun, one of the things I want to say is, "I work." It's not that I don't have outside interests; it's just that at CCC we're not sure when the fun stops and the work begins, or when the work stops and the fun begins. Eric likes to call what we do "recess." Maybe now you get the idea.

We have a pond outside our "Big Yellow Box" facility. It's not a lake, just a cold, murky pond with no fountain. The Student Community staff members were taking a break from their staff retreat when one of them had the fun idea to have everyone swim across the pond — in their street clothes! So after two screaming laps *running around* the pond, the whole team began *swimming across* the pond. Keep in mind, this was no warm July day. The air temperature was about 50 degrees. Once they jumped in the pond, their screams stopped "cold" and were replaced by flailing arms and legs responding to the shocking reality of hypothermia. It just seemed like fun in the moment.

> When people ask me what I do for fun, one of the things I want to say is, "I work." It's not that I don't have outside interests; it's just that at CCC we're not sure when the fun stops and the work begins, or when the work stops and the fun begins.

Yes, we like to have fun!

With our offices overlooking the "gymatorium" (a cross between a gym and an auditorium), we find it tough to resist the urge to go downstairs and shoot some hoops from time to time. However, on one occasion a friendly game of "horse" got ugly. About five staffers in street clothes were shooting around when somebody threw down the gauntlet: "Half-court shots — last person to make one has to run through the café and offices with his shirt off." How do you respond to a challenge of that nature? Like any red-blooded (and male) pastor, you accept. Carter Moss, the newest of our campus pastors, came out on the short end of this stick, failing to sink a half-court shot after multiple tries. He's still trying to explain to his wife how this picture of him running shirtless through the halls of the Big Yellow Box appeared on my blog.

After I posted Carter's picture on my blog, I asked people to submit captions. Here are a few comments that came from people all across the country:

- "Nobody's looking ... nobody's looking ... nobody's looking ..."
- "Someday this will make a great sermon illustration ... uh, but not right now!"
- "I'm trying to start a new fad at CCC — 'No Shirt Sunday.'"

A few other examples of our "fun":

- *Quote wall.* A quote wall displayed in our office features random sayings heard by staff people through the course of our working together. More than anything, it is intended to poke fun at the staff person quoted and bring puzzled looks to the faces of volunteers who walk into our office.
- *Stuffed animals.* Several years ago our staff worked through Jim Collins's book *Good to Great.* If you're familiar with his book, you know that he has developed what he calls the Hedgehog model to help companies and churches clarify their mission and core business. When we started working through the

book, we bought everyone on staff a stuffed hedgehog. Little did we know that when you squeeze them they make a very high-pitched (and very annoying) sound. Need I say more?

- *Food.* Our implicit curriculum tends to place a high value on food. I wish I could say we value healthy food, but that's not always the case. It's a rare meeting that doesn't include food. Our creative arts teams meet every Tuesday morning for breakfast on site. The menu includes such delicacies as Fruit Loops, Pop-Tarts, and chocolate milk. It's all organic, of course.

- *Sharing the credit and benefit.* If this book actually sells, you can help us have even more fun. We've already determined that 50 percent of the income will be put in a staff "fun fund." This decision reflects the value we place on collaboration and fun. We know that the knowledge and experience expressed in these pages (insert joke here) didn't come only from the people with their names on the cover, so why not share the credit and the benefit?

When you create a fun work environment, people want to come to work because they enjoy it. As a result, productivity increases, and you'll be more likely to retain gifted staff people because they can't imagine working anywhere else. And in the meantime, you're creating memories that will last a lifetime.

SECRET IDEA 5: COMPETITION

"This week has to be better than last week."

At our last all-staff meeting, I was discussing the tension that we constantly feel between reproducing at all levels and delivering consistent quality. To illustrate my point, I asked our "Northern Hemisphere" pastors to face off with our "Southern Hemisphere" pastors in a friendly game of tug-of-war. Afterward, John Ciesniewski, who represented our Southern Hemisphere, was heard asking, "How do you know when you've messed up your sciatic nerve?" Eeek. We're a very competitive group.

I'm on the teaching team at CCC with my brother, Jon (need I say more about competition?), and Tim Sutherland, one of the most gifted communicators on the planet. When Tim or Jon hit a home run during a weekend celebration service, completely engaging the congregation, and people are motivated toward life change, I can't help but feel some competition, maybe even a little insecurity. At that point I have two options: (1) I can be jealous and wish I could engage and motivate people the way they did last week, or (2) I can go to work on developing my skills so that I can more effectively engage the congregation myself.

Another example: When we're sitting in the Big Idea meeting and one of my teammates is coming up with creative idea after creative idea while I remain silent, either I can be frustrated that my idea well seems to be running dry, or I can work harder next time to come to the meeting with more ideas or, better yet, ask my teammate what he or she is doing to be so well prepared for the meeting. Competition is a good thing. It can be tremendously motivating, and surrounding yourself with capable people breeds healthy competition.

> When Tim or Jon hit a home run during a weekend celebration service, completely engaging the congregation, and people are motivated toward life change, I can't help but feel some competition, maybe even a little insecurity.

One advantage of having multiple locations implementing the Big Idea is that we have numerous labs in which to experiment with a variety of ideas. When a new site is launched, we all benefit from the innovations discovered through that launch. We told you about our weekly survey filled out by our staff and key leaders, ranking the effectiveness of our services and ministries for a given weekend. We debrief these scores at a weekly catalyst review meeting. It's one way we measure our progress. It's also a way for us to measure ourselves against each other.

We also keep track of how well we are developing 3C Christ followers with our 3CMS (church management software) database. Tools like the survey, the database, and the catalyst review meeting help us to learn from each other in terms of how each of us is recruiting and developing artists and leaders to execute the Big Idea. Sure, there are times when one campus may feel as though it's falling behind. But in our environment, if you aggressively seek out answers and resolutions, you'll find that many people are ready and willing to share ideas.

Here are four keys that have helped us create healthy competition among our staff and campuses:

1. *Hire the best.* We have a tremendously talented team. Most of them not only welcome competition but thrive on it. Highly competent people will find healthy competition to be very motivating.

2. *Keep score.* We've all heard it before: "You count what counts." If you value attendance, chances are you're keeping track of attendance. If you value conversion growth, you've more than likely put processes in place to track that growth. We value 3C Christ followers who celebrate, connect, and contribute. We track the 3Cs diligently, and we welcome healthy competition in these areas.

3. *Celebrate "wins" with everyone.* Almost all of our meetings begin with the question, "Where are we winning?" It's a great opportunity for us to catch someone doing something right and tell everyone about it. It's also a great way to communicate where you see God at work in your own life and ministry.

4. *Celebrate the collective "wins" more than the individual wins.* Look for places where the entire team is winning and celebrate those wins. Occasionally, our campuses will compete

as we compare attendance, number of baptisms, number of new groups, and so on. However, most of our competition is against ourselves as we compare our collective progress over the past few months or years.

SECRET IDEA 6: "YES"

"Just when you're about to say, 'Why?' think, 'Why not?'"

In an article in *Fast Company* titled "My Greatest Lesson," Katherine Hudson writes, "When someone offers you a challenge, don't think of all the reasons why you can't do it. Instead, say, 'Yes!' Then figure out how you'll get it done."[6]

At CCC, we have said yes to a lot of things that we had no clue how to do:

- Partner with a real estate developer to create a church-centered community.
- Start a new campus in a community where a large percentage of the population doesn't speak English.
- Write a book!

Foolish? Some would say yes. But we have learned that if we want to be involved in innovative and creative new things, we have to "lead with a yes." "Lead with a yes" is a common saying among the Community Christian Church staff. Sure, there are times when leading with a yes gets us in over our heads. But far more often, it allows us to be part of new and exciting ventures that help us better accomplish our mission. Peter Block makes this point in his book *The Answer to How Is Yes.*[7] How do you change the culture of your organization or church so that it is innovative and creative? The answer is to respond to opportunities with a yes.

Leading with a yes is an important part of the implicit curriculum that makes the Big Idea process work. The "yes" mindset gives outrageous, seemingly impossible ideas a chance to live and breathe and sometimes be implemented in whole or in part. The "no" mindset refuses to give any outside-the-box idea a chance to live and stifles innovation and creative collaboration.

If you want to be a more innovative person or create a culture of innovation in your organization, try a few of these:

- *Develop a yes reflex.* Most of us have a no reflex to new and creative ideas that seem impossible. But you can change this; practice saying yes to your kids, spouse, and friends. Leading with a yes can be learned and can be taught to a whole organization. So the next time someone brings up a new opportunity, make sure the first word that comes out of your mouth is *yes*.

> **The yes mindset gives outrageous, seemingly impossible ideas a chance to live and breathe and sometimes be implemented in whole or in part.**

Recently one of our directors met with a church in our area that was interested in pursuing an unusual partnership with CCC. The staff person asked me, "What should I tell them?" I said, "Well, at this point, just keep saying yes until there's good reason to say no." Unfortunately, we often operate in reverse. We lean toward saying no until there is good reason to say yes, and as a result, opportunities don't come our way because we have been too quick to say no.

- *"Yes" gives you more time to figure it out.* Training yourself to have a yes reflex doesn't commit you to actually implementing the idea. Before "Yes" ever commits you to doing something, it actually buys you time to figure out how you are going to make it happen. Often we say yes and then take time to regroup and consider the opportunity's potential benefits and liabilities. Leading with a yes gives you time to figure out if you can really pull it off.

When a small group of key leaders from a church in Montgomery approached CCC's leadership about establishing a new location at their facility, we led with a yes. After much prayer, conversation, and dreaming, God led us to launch a campus there, and now close to six hundred people celebrate there every week. I found out later that at least two other churches and another church planting organization led with a no and missed out on the opportunity.

- *There is always time to say, "Not yet."* If you have a no reflex, you rob yourself of the time to talk about the idea and figure out if the impossible is possible. But if you lead with a yes, you give yourself the time you need to discuss and explore how to make it happen. If, after giving the idea careful consideration, you decide it's not possible at this time, you can still come back and say, "We talked about the possibility, and we love the idea — just not yet."

- *"Not yet" is always better than "No."* I've always preferred "Not yet" to "No." My son insists that his parents have developed a wide range of ways to respond to the onslaught of childhood requests that simply put off the inevitable "No." If you ask him, he'll tell you that if "Yes" is on one side of the continuum and "No" is on the other, somewhere in the middle is "I don't know." Between "I don't know" and "Yes" are responses such as "Probably," "Maybe," "I think so." Between "I don't know" and "No" are less-affirmative responses such as, "We'll see," "I doubt it," and the ever-hated "Probably not." Why not develop this same range of responses when it comes to leadership? Often we are too quick to say "Probably not" or "No" rather than "Maybe" or "We'll see" or even "Not yet." And "No" eliminates the potential of any future "Yes." It squelches creativity and demotivates the asker.

We're not making a case for having no boundaries; we're describing how innovation happens. And innovation happens in places where "No" is seldom heard and "Not yet" is preferred to "No." "Not yet" keeps the opportunity alive and keeps people thinking and improving their ideas.

PART FOUR

● ● ● ●

A Really Big Idea

CHAPTER 12

CREATING AND REPRODUCING BIG IDEA NETWORKS

The launch team was gathering for its first meeting. In a matter of days the new church would go public with its very first worship service. It was definitely an emerging church, but you could also say that it was seeker targeted. The members of the launch team didn't know much about church growth, but they were completely pro-numbers even though they were organized around a house church model. All kinds of people made up the launch team: those who were gungho and those who would give up; leaders and followers; the wealthy and the unemployed; men, women, and children. It wasn't the most gifted or best resourced of new church plants, but it did have one thing that every new church needs: a certainty about its mission.

JESUS' REALLY BIG IDEA

Jesus cast the vision for this emerging, seeker-targeted house church, and he relayed a really Big Idea: "You will receive power when the Holy Spirit comes on you; and you will be my witnesses in Jerusalem, and in all Judea and Samaria, and to the ends of the earth" (Acts 1:8).

As the disciples listened to Jesus, one word stood out glaringly: "witnesses." When this group of spiritual entrepreneurs heard him say, "You will be my witnesses," they didn't think he meant "sharing

185

their story" or "inviting people into a small group." What they heard him say was *marturios*, and they knew that word meant "martyr." The one thing that stuck in the hearts and heads of those members of the launch team was that starting this local church would be a huge risk—and it might even cost them their lives.

Challenge 1: Take Bold Risks
"And you will be my witnesses."

When we started Community Christian Church, I was twenty-five and my brother, Jon, was twenty-three. Basically the venture was a huge risk that we and three friends decided to take. We had no money, no people, no facility, and no sense! We just wanted to help people find their way back to God. That was over fifteen years ago, but time, size, or perceived success does not change the challenge that is before us. We are still a launch team and we are still called to be witnesses, *marturios*, to risk it all for the cause of Christ.

> We are still a launch team and we are still called to be witnesses, *marturios*, to risk it all for the cause of Christ.

We just added our eighth CCC location. This site is in the Pilsen neighborhood of Chicago, where 95 percent of the population is Latino and the first language is Spanish. We knew that starting another CCC location in this community would mean translating our Big Idea into Spanish. So why would a predominately Anglo, English-speaking, upper-middle-class, suburban megachurch risk a string of successes and start a location in Pilsen? Because we are still a launch team that has been challenged by Jesus to take risks that may cost us everything.

Challenge 2: Be Spirit-Led
"You will receive power when the Holy Spirit comes on you."

There was no mistaking what Jesus meant by *marturios*, but many of the disciples had to be scratching their heads when Jesus explained that the "Holy Spirit" would guide this risk-taking endeavor. How was the first launch team to make sense of that?

When the Bieritz family first contacted me with their offer to give us a facility and property on Montgomery Road, I kept the information pretty quiet while we discussed the possibility as a lead team. I just wasn't sure God's Spirit was leading us this way as a church. But the day I presented the possibility to our staff members and asked them to pray about it, I was sure God's Spirit was leading us to Montgomery! We had just finished our all-staff meeting, and not long after I returned to my desk, I received the following email from Sherry, one of our staff members who had been in that meeting:

Dave,

Weird thing — I had a dream last night. It was weird because what stood out to me was this little old lady standing there telling me that I needed to go and find this church in Montgomery. I kept asking her how to get there and she told me to go down Montgomery Road and I would see the signs and they would tell me where to go. She said I couldn't miss it, but it was important that I check it out. Then I hear about this church thing today with this property that someone wants to give us in Montgomery? On Montgomery Road? Weird, isn't it?

Sherry

That was a God-thing. Sherry's dream was confirmation from God that we were to start a Montgomery campus in that old church building the Bieritz family gave us. We closed down the old church in the fall. We literally had a memorial service for the former church. We invited the twenty or so members and friends and celebrated what God had done during the church's 163-year history. Then we rehabbed the building, expanded the parking lot, and prepared for a grand opening. On the first weekend more than six hundred people packed into a little building that hadn't seen more than forty in years! It was a Spirit-led adventure.

As I look back on what God has done and is doing through Community Christian Church and the NewThing Network, I wish we had a better strategic plan. I really do! But so far we consistently find ourselves responding to the Spirit's leading. It feels risky and sometimes disorganized. But it's just as Jesus told his disciples: "You will receive power when the Holy Spirit comes on you." He was explaining that this risk-taking endeavor called church planting would be Spirit-led. It may not have made complete sense to that first launch team at the time, but over the next few months and years they would come to know that the risks they would take on this mission would always be Spirit-led.

As I look back on what God has done and is doing through Community Christian Church and the NewThing Network, I wish we had a better strategic plan. I really do! But so far we consistently find ourselves responding to the Spirit's leading. It feels risky and sometimes disorganized.

Challenge 3: Continually Reproduce

"In Jerusalem, and in all Judea and Samaria, and to the ends of the earth."

When a church responds to Jesus' first two challenges and continually takes Spirit-led risks, its people will find that he will increase their influence in expanding concentric circles ("Jerusalem … Judea … Samaria … the ends of the earth"). In 1998 we were one church in one location with two services and eight hundred attenders. But when God's Spirit created the possibility and we took the risk to go multisite, we began reproducing more and more sites. Over the next eight years we expanded our influence to eight locations, twenty-plus services, and more than five thousand attenders.

And I thought it might stop there — but that was just the beginning! In 2002 thirty-five of our people moved from Chicago to Denver to plant a new church. And over the next couple of years, we launched churches in Bakersfield (California), Detroit, Manhattan, and Boston that are all part of our NewThing Network.

This summer, between the completion of this book and its release, my daughter and I will get on a plane bound for Africa. I've never been to Africa, and a part of me would prefer to stay home and manage the last Little League game of the season. And over the next nine months we are sending several of our staff people on exploratory trips to Africa, Asia, Central America, and Europe. Why are we all taking trips to the ends of the earth? Because we are still a launch team and we are still obeying the challenge of Jesus.

Many in that first launch team had not explored far beyond the boundaries of Jerusalem. And now Jesus was telling them that this great adventure would be led by someone they couldn't see, would cost them all they could see, and would take them places they'd never been! That's Jesus' really Big Idea for every church. It's not enough for our churches to simply teach a Big Idea to our people. Our churches must be living out the really Big Idea of Jesus. And his really Big Idea was that his church would be a risk-taking, Spirit-led, reproducing church. Is it possible for your church to be that kind of church? Absolutely!

> Every church goes through four developmental stages on its way to accomplishing this really Big Idea.

How could your church live out this really Big Idea of being a risk-taking, Spirit-led, reproducing church?

Every church goes through four developmental stages on its way to accomplishing this really Big Idea.

Phase 1: A Really Big Idea Church

A "really Big Idea church" is a church led by Christ followers who believe that Jesus' Acts 1:8 vision is not merely hypothetical but possible! It is a community that willingly takes radical risks that could cost them everything. It is a church constantly on the lookout for the places God's Spirit will take it next. The people of this church pray to fulfill Jesus' vision by reproducing in expanding concentric circles just as he described: "Jerusalem … Judea … Samaria … the ends of the earth."

When we launched Community Christian Church, we had no money, no facilities, and no people; but the one thing we did have was Jesus' really Big Idea. That really Big Idea led us to develop a vision that we prayed would occur over time in three moves:

Move 1: Impact church
Move 2: Reproducing church
Move 3: Movement of reproducing churches

Phase 2: A Reproducing Church

A reproducing church is a church that is advancing the mission of Jesus by moving beyond its own personal "Jerusalem." This church has reproduced Christ followers by adding a new site or planting new churches. Motivated by God's Spirit, this church has taken risks to reproduce itself in other communities.

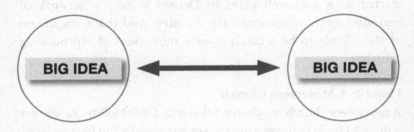

Before Community Christian Church had its first facility, we added a second CCC site in a community fifteen miles south. It was the first of the eight sites we now have and the beginning of a "new thing" that God was doing as we became a reproducing church.

Phase 3: A Network Church
A network church is a church that is moving step-by-step with Jesus and seeing his really Big Idea reproduced in "Judea and Samaria." Spirit-motivated risk taking has brought this church to a place where it is now leading a network of churches that are out to fulfill Jesus' really Big Idea.

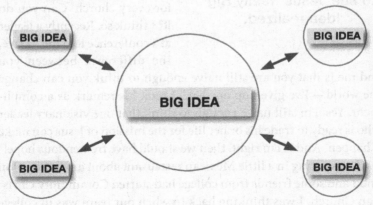

After eleven years chasing this really Big Idea of Jesus, we launched the NewThing Network (www.newthing.org). What started with a church plant in Denver is now a network of reproducing churches across the country. And that's the dream of NewThing: to be a catalyst for a movement of reproducing churches.

Phase 4: A Movement Church

A movement church is a church filled with Christ followers who are willing to trade their very lives to see Jesus' really Big Idea realized. This church moves far beyond "Jerusalem," even beyond "Judea and Samaria," and sees God's Spirit move it to "the ends of the earth." This church is so used by God that it is able to reproduce not just sites or churches but networks of reproducing churches.

The dream of everyone at Community Christian Church and the NewThing Network is to look back one day on the "good work" that God has done through us and know that we were used by his Spirit to help initiate a movement of people who found their way back to God.

> A movement church is a church filled with Christ followers who are willing to trade their very lives to see Jesus' really Big Idea realized.

That's Jesus' really Big Idea for every church. Can you do it? I think so. Recently a leader at a conference told me, "Dave, the difference between you and me is that you are still naive enough to think you can change the world — I've given up on that." I took his remark as a compliment. Yes, I'm still naive enough to think that one visionary leader who is ready to trade his or her life for the mission of Jesus can make it happen. And if I'm right, then we should have tremendous hope!

I was sitting in a little Mexican restaurant about a year after Jon and I and some friends from college had started Community Christian Church. I was thinking back to when our team was in college a few years before, dreaming of reaching our hometown, Chicago. Now, we knew that we could never reach all eight million people with one location, but what if we could divide and conquer? If we divided up, maybe we could reach the whole city. I had a map of Chicago on the bulletin board in my dorm room. We'd divided the city into four quadrants, with each of our initials on one of the four sections. It looked something like this:

Sure, the plan was a bit grandiose—but why not? Just thinking about those college days got me dreaming again. So I laid out a napkin on the table and started to sketch Chicago and the surrounding areas. Then I drew circles rather than quadrants, each representing the site of a new church. I stared at it. Then I took that napkin and tucked it into my day planner. And it stayed in that day planner for the next four years.

It stayed there until I had breakfast with a man named Larry, a very successful entrepreneur who had started several businesses. During breakfast Larry asked me, "So, Dave, what is the dream?

If you could do anything, what would you do?" To me, that is a very personal question. But he asked me again, "Dave, what is the dream?"

For the first time in four years, I pulled out that napkin, showed it to him, and said, "If I could do anything, this is what I'd do." Then Larry said something that was simple but absolutely life changing: "You can do it!" For me, everything changed in that moment. How powerful it was to have someone look me in the eye and listen to my heartfelt dream and then say with absolute confidence, "You can do it!"

> But if there's one thing I want you to remember, it's that simple and powerful phrase, "You can do it!"

CONCLUSION

We've covered a lot of Big Ideas in this book: the Big Idea of being a Christ follower and not a Christian; the Big Idea of living out Jesus' mission and not simply looking for more information; the Big Idea of being part of a movement by creating missional velocity. We've learned how your church can become a "B," "I," or "G" Big Idea church. We've examined how your church can develop and implement the Big Idea. And we've been challenged by the really Big Idea of Jesus. But if there's one thing I want you to remember, it's that simple and powerful phrase, "You can do it!"

APPENDIX

WWW.BIGIDEAONLINE.ORG/RESOURCES

Check out this link to get sample Big Idea resources:

- The Big Idea Discussion Guide
- The Big Idea Message Manuscript
- The Big Idea Service Flow Map
- The Big Idea student resources
- The Big Idea children's resources
- The Big Idea Planning Worksheet
- Other Big Idea resources

NOTES

Chapter 1: No More Christians!

1. Haddon Robinson, *Biblical Preaching* (Grand Rapids: Baker Academic, 2001), 35.

2. Thomas E. Patterson, *The Vanishing Voter* (New York: Knopf, 2002), 84.

3. Don Everts, *Jesus with Dirty Feet: A Down-to-Earth Look at Christianity for the Curious and Skeptical* (Downers Grove, IL: Intervarsity, 1999), 14 – 16. Taken from "Jesus with Dirty Feet" by Don Everts. Copyright © 1999 by Don Everts and InterVarsity Christian Fellowship/USA. Used with permission of InterVarsity Press, PO Box 1400, Downers Grove, IL 60515. www.ivpress.com.

Chapter 2: Communities of Transformation, Not Information

1. Tom McCann, "Corpse Discovered after Four Years," *Chicago Tribune*, May 10, 2001, 1.

2. Randy Frazee, *Making Room for Life: Trading Chaotic Lifestyles for Connected Relationships* (Grand Rapids: Zondervan, 2004), 33.

3. Gilbert Bilezikian, *Community 101: Reclaiming the Church as Community of Oneness* (Grand Rapids: Zondervan, 1997), 54.

Chapter 3: Creating Missional Velocity

1. Bill Hybels, *Courageous Leadership* (Grand Rapids: Zondervan, 2002), 63.

Chapter 4: The Genius of the "And"

1. Jim Collins and Jerry I. Porras, *Built to Last: Successful Habits of Visionary Companies* (New York: HarperCollins Essentials, 1994), 44 – 45.

2. Barry Schwartz, *The Paradox of Choice: Why More Is Less* (New York: HarperCollins, 2004), 3.

3. Warren Bennis, *Organizing Genius: The Secrets of Creative Collaboration* (Cambridge, MA: Perseus, 1997), 14.

4. Peter Drucker, *Innovation and Entrepreneurship* (New York: HarperCollins, 1985), 34.

5. Patrick Lencioni, *The Five Dysfunctions of a Team: A Leadership Fable* (San Francisco, Jossey-Bass, 2002), 188.

6. Andy Stanley, Reggie Joiner, and Lane Jones, *Seven Practices of Effective Ministry* (Sisters, OR: Multnomah, 2004), 122.

Chapter 6: Creating Your One-Year Big Idea Plan

1. Jim Collins, *Good to Great: Why Some Companies Make the Leap ... and Others Don't* (New York: HarperCollins, 2001), 121–22.

Chapter 8: The Two Most Important Players in the Big Idea

1. Patrick Lencioni, *The Five Dysfunctions of a Team: A Leadership Fable* (San Francisco: Jossey-Bass, 2002), 195.

Chapter 10: The Big Idea Teaching Team Meeting

1. Stanley Hauerwas, *Unleashing the Scripture: Freeing the Bible from Captivity to America* (Nashville: Abingdon Press, 1993), 31.

2. Rob Bell, "Crafting an Experience," *Preaching Today*, www.preachingtoday.com/16832.

Chapter 11: The Implicit Big Idea

1. Tom McGehee, *Whoosh: Business in the Fast Lane* (Cambridge, MA: Perseus, 2001).

2. Warren Bennis, *Organizing Genius: The Secrets of Creative Collaboration* (Cambridge, MA: Perseus, 1997), 204.

3. Jim Collins, *Good to Great: Why Some Companies Make the Leap ... and Others Don't* (New York: HarperCollins, 2001), 22.

4. Henry Cloud, *Nine Things You Simply Must Do to Succeed in Love and Life* (Brentwood, TN: Integrity, 2004), 201.

5. Kevin Freiberg and Jackie Freiberg, *Nuts! Southwest Airlines' Crazy Recipe for Business and Personal Success* (New York: Bard Press, 1996), 205.

6. Katherine Hudson, "My Greatest Lesson," *Fast Company* (June 1998), 83.

7. Peter Block, *The Answer to How Is Yes: Acting On What Matters* (San Francisco: Berrett-Koehler, 2001).

Dave Ferguson is the lead pastor of Community Christian Church (www.communitychristian.org), an innovative multisite missional community that is passionate about "helping people find their way back to God." CCC has grown from Dave, his wife, and four friends to over 5000 people meeting every weekend in eight locations. CCC empowers over 600 volunteer leaders to oversee difference-making ministry throughout Chicago and was recently recognized as one of the most influential churches in America. Dave provides visionary leadership for the NewThing Network (www.newthing.org), whose dream is to be "a catalyst for a movement of reproducing churches." NewThing is a network of reproducing churches internationally and a resource to churches looking to reproduce multiple sites or new churches. Dave is also the cofounder of and serves on the board of directors for the Institute for Community (www.instituteforcommunity.org), which partners with real-estate developers to accomplish the mission of "helping people build quality relationships where you live and work through the power of genuine community." Next to Jesus, Dave loves his wife, Sue, the most, and then his three terrific kids, Amy, Joshua, and Caleb. If you want to keep up with Dave's adventures, check out his blog (www.daveferguson.org).

Jon Ferguson is the cofounder of Community Christian Church. He plays a key role in identifying and developing small group leaders, coaches, and staff personnel. He serves as teaching pastor and leads and directs all Community ministries (small groups for children through adults). Jon is the cofounder and executive director of NewThing Network. NewThing (www.newthing.org) is a mission of Community Christian Church with a vision to be a catalyst for a movement of reproducing churches. In addition to its network of reproducing churches, NewThing serves thousands of churches through its conferences, coaching, and creative resources. He also serves on the boards of the Church Planting Network, the Institute for Community, and Stadia East. He resides in Naperville with his wife, Lisa, and their two children, Graham and Chloe. He maintains a blog at www.jonferguson.org.

Eric Bramlett has been the creative arts director for Community Christian Church since 1996. Eric's background is in professional theater, and he holds degrees in acting and directing. He is responsible for overseeing all large-group experiences from intensive artistic vision through production. Eric continues to be involved in the Chicago theater scene, most notably as an Artistic Associate for Porchlight Music Theatre Chicago, a theater company he has been associated with since its inception in 1995. Eric lives in Naperville, Illinois, with his wife, Kristi, and their three children, Sadie, Dillon, and Anna.

About the Leadership Network Innovation Series

Since 1984, Leadership Network has fostered church innovation and growth by diligently pursuing its far-reaching mission statement: *To identify high-capacity Christian leaders, to connect them with other leaders, and to help them multiply their impact.*

While specific techniques may vary as the church faces new opportunities and challenges, Leadership Network consistently focuses on bringing together entrepreneurial leaders who are pursuing similar ministry initiatives. The resulting peer-to-peer interaction, dialogue, and collaboration—often across denominational lines—helps these leaders better refine their individual strategies and accelerate their own innovations.

To further enhance this process, Leadership Network develops and distributes highly targeted ministry tools and resources, including books, DVDs and videotapes, special reports, e-publications, and free downloads.

Launched in 2006, the Leadership Network Innovation Series presents case studies and insights from leading practitioners and pioneering churches that are successfully navigating the ever-changing streams of spiritual renewal in modern society. Each book offers *real* stories, about *real* leaders, in *real* churches, doing *real* ministry. Readers gain honest and thorough analyses, transferable principles, and clear guidance on how to put proven ideas to work in their individual settings.

With the assistance of Leadership Network—and the Leadership Network Innovation Series—today's Christian leaders are energized, equipped, inspired, and enabled to multiply their own dynamic kingdom-building initiatives. And the pace of innovative ministry is growing as never before.

For additional information on the mission or activities of Leadership Network, please contact:

LEADERSHIP ✖ NETWORK˙

800-765-5323 • www.leadnet.org • client.care@leadnet.

Share Your Thoughts

With the Author: Your comments will be forwarded to
the author when you send them to *zauthor@zondervan.com*.

With Zondervan: Submit your review of this book
by writing to *zreview@zondervan.com*.

Free Online Resources at
www.zondervan.com

Zondervan AuthorTracker: Be notified whenever your favorite
authors publish new books, go on tour, or post an update
about what's happening in their lives at www.zondervan.com/
authortracker.

Daily Bible Verses and Devotions: Enrich your life with daily
Bible verses or devotions that help you start every morning
focused on God. Visit www.zondervan.com/newsletters.

Free Email Publications: Sign up for newsletters on Christian
living, academic resources, church ministry, fiction, children's
resources, and more. Visit www.zondervan.com/newsletters.

Zondervan Bible Search: Find and compare Bible passages in
a variety of translations at www.zondervanbiblesearch.com.

Other Benefits: Register yourself to receive online benefits
like coupons and special offers, or to participate in research.